NOT JUST SPIRITUAL

NOT JUST SPIRITUAL

MY JOURNEY FROM PERSONAL RELIGION TO THE CATHOLIC FAITH

CHRISTINE FLYNN

Published by Catholic Answers, Inc.
2020 Gillespie Way
El Cajon, California 92020
1-888-291-8000 orders
619-387-0042 fax
catholic.com

Printed in the United States of America

Cover design by ebooklaunch.com
Interior design by Claudine Mansour Design

978-1-68357-378-4
978-1-68357-379-1 Kindle
978-1-68357-380-7 ePub

To my husband Pat,
for taking me with him to Christ.

Contents

This is a true story.
Names have been changed to protect privacy.

Prologue

People living in deep sin are not always the ones who are most in need of our help, but rather the people who think they're doing well, when in actuality the opposite is true.

Before my conversion to Catholicism, I was that person—outwardly functioning but spiritually sick. I considered myself to be a "good person." I opened doors for strangers, volunteered, gave blood, recycled bottles and cans, and limited my consumption of plastic goods. I once drove all over town in the middle of the night looking for an emergency-care veterinarian because a stray cat was dying on my front porch and I didn't want her to suffer. That, I figured, certainly tipped the karmic scales in my favor.

I never did anything especially depraved, not by today's standards. No murders or drunk-driving accidents. I wasn't mean to people, and I enjoyed a nice relationship with my family. My vices were small and harmless. Co-workers laughed at my sneaking in late and slipping out of work early without the boss knowing, friends giggled at my retelling of casual sexual escapades, and boyfriends certainly didn't complain about the use of pornography. My white lies either embellished stories to make them more amusing or kept other people from getting their feelings unnecessarily hurt. And if I used marijuana in my teens, it was just a tool to help me process the difficulties of life.

I had my own moral code, which was simply to live my best life without actively hurting other people. And if I *did* hurt other people? Well, that was more a symptom of where they were in their own life rather than a reflection of what I had done to them.

Looking back now, it's plain to see that my self-image, my actions, and my morality were in deep contradiction to one another. How highly I thought of myself in no way reflected how I acted, and how I acted in no way aligned with anything but my subjective and changeable whims.

I know I was not unique or even special. Millions live as I did—deep in denial, functioning but spiritually sick, in a life of contradiction. Rarer, though, are those who are led to acknowledge that contradiction and rise from it. And that is how God led me.

For a long time, I didn't see or accept how sick I had become. With just a little massaging, I could justify all my sins. The lie I told my mother? It protected her from knowing about the things I felt I had under control that she would needlessly worry over. The job I randomly stopped showing up for? The company would now be able to hire an employee who cared more than I did. The abortion I had at seventeen? An unfortunate necessity. Besides, when it came down to it, any of the things I did or experienced were all part of my *spiritual journey*. None of it could be "wrong" because I was working toward my ultimate end: becoming a beautifully realized spirit unchained by the prison of my physical self. Surely, a journey such as that couldn't always be pretty or fun, especially for people who got in my way.

My beliefs (I hesitate to group them into a "system," which would imply some sort of structure) were steeped almost entirely in emotion. No one could tell me what to do. I envisioned myself as a wild and free horse, untamable, and determined to reinvent everything to keep myself that way. Much of what you'll read in the coming pages may appear to not make sense. I could believe something totally absurd one minute, and then if pushed to make a commitment, I could change to the exact opposite position. For the moral relativist, this flip-flopping is often the case. So if it seems crazy to you ("How could anyone believe *that*?"), don't try to puzzle it out. Know that I did believe crazy things and acted on them, and there are others who do as well.

I wish I could say that my shortcomings could be chalked up to peer pressure or the sins of youth, but truthfully, plenty of my friends were leading more wholesome lives than I. My poor choices continued into my thirties, even after I'd gotten married and had children—when I had "grown up." The sins weren't as dramatic then, but they were insidious. I was settled comfortably into a life of egotism, arrogance, and isolationism, based almost entirely on whatever emotion I felt in any given moment.

I followed my feelings and did basically whatever I wanted, so long as it wasn't obviously atrocious, and my life choices reflected this selfishness. Despite my desire to understand my purpose and the ultimate meaning of life, I rejected any organized religion that might offer answers to my questions, instead favoring spirituality, where I could create my own Religion of One—in which I was both God and worshiper.

For those leading the "spiritual-but-not-religious" life—whether looking for answers in stars or crystals or dreams as I did or seeking some other secret source of wisdom—riding emotions seemed like a quick and comfortable solution. Whether we hold stock in reincarnation or annihilationism, nirvana or naturalism, or if we believe

Christ is a mythical character in a great cosmic play or if we refuse to acknowledge him at all, we devise our private piecemeal religions to keep suffering away, to elevate us beyond this valley of tears, to make sense of the pain we see and feel in this fallen world.

What my younger self did not understand is that our desire to make sense of suffering, to understand the world around us, and hope in something greater, only exists because there really *is* something greater; *the* Greatest Good—God, who gives us the gift of that desire to draw us closer to him and enable us to know him. "Our hearts are restless until they rest in thee," wrote St. Augustine. He couldn't have been more right. Our restlessness directs us to know, love, and serve the Lord, and once there, we can find rest under his easy yoke. But stewing in this restlessness for too long, without any ultimate aim, without the guideposts that the religion of truth offers us, can cause despair and hopelessness. The burden here becomes onerous and damning.

How we respond to that gift determines whether we are right or wrong. Do we allow our emotions to rule us, to drive us to seek relief from pain despite being thrust deeper into the darkness, and to live in the restlessness out of which God calls us? Or do we allow truth and love to bring us into a lasting relationship with the One who created us?

This question, whether we acknowledge it or not, affects a growing number of people. A quarter of Americans consider themselves "spiritual," but say they aren't interested in religion. Practicing a specific set of rituals or attending gatherings just isn't important to them. Another fifth don't want anything to do with either spirituality or religion.[1] These aren't small percentages, and long has our society reflected these beliefs, which can be utterly disheartening.

If my story can do anything, I hope that can show that there is hope, even for the most stalwart of the anti-religious set. God draws us to him, and even someone as stubborn and selfish as me can be drawn in. He is doing great things in our fallen world, and if through a part of my story, he moves you or a loved one to be transformed too, thanks be to God! With him, there are satisfying, wonderful, beautiful answers that our restless hearts naturally seek.

NOT JUST SPIRITUAL

CHAPTER 1

A Catholic–Curious Youth

Before construction crews came and bulldozed the forest behind my parents' house into a flat expanse of red clay, there were winding paths, trampled by deer and children, through the soft pine and rocky undergrowth. They led, like the curving tunnels of an ant farm, into a wooded dreamland ripe for any child's imagination, with a creek edged by bluebells that magically appeared each spring, treasures deposited by a tornado that had once ripped through the neighborhood, as well as foundations of houses long abandoned and old stone huts used to dry tobacco leaves. We kids dubbed it the "Way Back," and it was perfect.

My best friend and I spent hours there imagining and playing. We had bedrooms tucked between rows of pine and a kitchen to stir up wild concoctions of bark and rocks and leaves. I didn't know much of anything about God; my understanding was limited to what I learned through movies like *The Ten Commandments*—a film I loved to watch each Easter while devouring candy buttons and coconut nests—and what I had read in the children's Bible from the sixties my aunt had gifted me. Fortunately, my Catholic friend knew about God. So at her request, in a tiny circle of trees, we set up a church, we worshipped God, and we prayed to Mary. In the Way Back, I had a distinct feeling that God was good. He made the woods that we played in and he made my best friend, so he had to be good. Having that space consecrated for him felt special and holy.

Without knowing it, we had what philosophers call a *sensus divinitatis*—a natural sense of the divine that drives humans to ask *Who are we?* and *Why are we here?* and *Where are we going?* This sense of the divine directs us, in each and every culture, regardless of geography or placement in time, to a belief in some transcendent being. Because of the world's imperfections, we're left to our own conclusions in a half-light. Our state of sin gives a muddled sense of God, even as he reveals himself to us.

At nine years old, I hadn't a clue about God's revelation, but my friend spoke of him with such certainty that I believed in him too.

Without guidance or direction, the spiritual certainty I had as a young child playing pretend in the woods began to dim. At first it wasn't anything catastrophic that took away my innate sense of God; but over time my childhood faith began to fall apart, piece-by-piece, like a puzzle that had been half-finished and then neglected. I remember snippets. Some were from my family, like being told to ignore anything I heard whenever I went to church with a friend or if we were "forced" to go to Mass by an elderly family member. I mentioned once that I might like to be a nun someday, to which I was simply told, "No, you don't!" I was extremely impressionable. Good or bad, I believed what I was told or what was implied about religion, which more often than not was referred to as "B.S."

When I was six, my New Yorker parents, with the literal and whimsical flip of a coin, decided to move to

North Carolina. We had recently spent several years in southern California, out in the sunshine, eating health food, and away from the Catholicism of my family's roots. I'd grown used to either a Yankee accent or Valley Girl uptalk. We had great bagels and avocados and a cool, cosmopolitan way of thinking. The Carolinas were . . . different. Pig-pickings, Confederate flags, businesses closed on Sundays, and a slow southern drawl.

Because of this cross-country move, I was suddenly confronted with religion for the first time in a very overt way. Christianity surrounded us. I learned what Sunday school was and that Jesus saved people. My upbringing up until that point hadn't included Christianity. Rather, the general consensus of the household was clear: organized religion was, at best, an unnecessary belief system that kept people intellectually sedated, and at worst, the root cause of most, if not all, the atrocities in human history. There was religion, and there was intelligence, and you couldn't have both.

I couldn't articulate that dichotomy until I was older, and later still before I understood that it is false.

Ironically, when I think back to my childhood, we could have made a great Christian family. Our home life was stable and loving. My parents never divorced. We spent a lot of time together, sharing meals and stories and laughter. I had, and still do have, a strong relationship with both my parents, who disciplined me out of love. The funny thing is, my parents created a home filled with the Christian values *they* were raised with, but decided not to pass on. Religion simply was a nonstarter, not just because of how it was addressed (or not) at home, but from what I experienced firsthand from the Christians among whom I now found myself.

Growing up in the South, there were three questions that every new person was asked:

1. Where are you from?
2. What does your daddy (or husband) do?
3. What church do you go to?

Preferably, the answers would go something like: (1) from somewhere south of the Mason-Dixon Line, (2) works for a local business, and (3) some Baptist or Evangelical congregation.

I, however, could answer none of these questions correctly. I was born in New York and moved to the South after spending four years on the weird West Coast; I actually wasn't quite sure what my dad did, but I was fairly certain it was doing some work for a foreign company. And church? Yeah, that was a big N.O. At first, I wasn't sure *why* we didn't go to church, but as the years went by, the farther removed from organized religion my parents—and by extension, I—became, an attitude compounded during our first few years in the South, as we were repeatedly told that we were going to hell when we couldn't nod in agreement when random people asked, "Have you accepted Jesus Christ as your personal Lord and Savior?"

A family down the street often told my mother that my brother and I were little devils. Another family in the neighborhood decorated their home with crosses but wouldn't let a black friend on their property. One group of Christians stood just off school property on warm days and chucked small Bibles into the open car windows of students leaving campus at the end of the day. And there was a time when nearly everyone seemed to wear those silicone WWJD ("What Would Jesus Do?") bracelets and treat Christ like a pop-culture chum who just wanted to hang out and listen to guitar worship music.

Over time, these attitudes helped cement in my head that Christians were hostile, hypocritical yokels.

The event that sealed my general dismissal of Christianity came in seventh grade at a slumber party. Most of the girls there were devout Southern Baptists, and then there was me and one other non-Christian, a girl who had Chinese roots. Who knows how, there in the basement in our pajamas, we got on the topic of the end of the world, but we did, and suddenly these girls were explaining in great detail the Rapture, and how, without Christ, nonbelievers—myself and my friend included—would be slaves of Satan for a thousand years.

"Just imagine," one girl said, "you're on an airplane and the Rapture happens. Half the passengers suddenly vanish, you don't know what's going on, and then . . . hell on Earth."

As it happened, my Chinese-American friend was flying to Asia the following week on a family trip, and the thought of being abandoned to the devil on an airplane proved too much. She started shaking and crying. And I, feeling like she was being bullied, told the other girls to stop. They wouldn't. A shouting match ensued and became so loud and passionate that the host mother stomped into the basement and told us she would have to call our parents to come pick us up if we didn't pipe down. That threat didn't work, and the other girl was so frightened that she was more than happy to cut short the slumber party and go home to spend time with her parents, given Jesus' seemingly imminent return interrupting the upcoming trip.

I hated all of it. If God was real, as these girls said he was, I couldn't believe he'd be so cruel as to bring a nice girl like my friend to tears. Those Christians were so confident, so sure in their beliefs, I had to ask, "Is this what Christianity is all about?" I had a few Mormon and Catholic and Jewish friends, but, by and large, the loudest, surest religious people I knew were those who lectured me about Jesus just so I'd know what I was missing when I got to hell.

Of course, during these formative years, I had other interactions with Christians that weren't quite so heated, but without a good understanding of who Christ was, their evangelism made no sense to me. I would occasionally get invited to go to Christian fellowship meetings in the gym after school, but it was only the promise of free pizza and soda that enticed me. After a while, even the draw of food lost its appeal because at some point we'd have to put down the slices and ping-pong paddles and listen to a motivational speaker who had been brought in to describe their life without Jesus, usually a degenerate person, in and out of jail, hooked on drugs, friendless, hopeless—in all respects, a failure at life—but who had an intense come-to-Jesus moment and was able to turn his or her life around by being born again in faith.

As a young girl who came from a "regular" family and who got good grades and had a nice social life, though, I felt I had nothing in common with these reformed losers. I was happy for them that they could turn themselves around and that this Jesus person helped them do that, but I was doing pretty well on my own. The dark underbelly of everyday life was far removed from my corner of the world. I had no intention of making the same horrible choices that had left them homeless, addicted, and prostituting themselves for the next fix.

If I could have summed up the person of Jesus back then, it would've been this: Jesus was for the weak. He could help the people who, through a series of mistakes and bad decisions, found themselves addicted to drugs or alcohol or sex or gambling and maybe were homeless and without family or friends. Or he was for people like my slumber-party friends, who seemed to swim in self-righteousness, feeding off a combination of their fear of hell and their delight that, as one of the "chosen," they would never wind up there.

I was wrong on both counts, but at the time, whether or not I knew much about Jesus or his life didn't matter as much as knowing that, based on the people I knew who claimed to follow him, he definitely wasn't for me. This conclusion solidified in my mind little more than a handful of years after those God-infused play sessions in the Way Back. I can see now just how obvious that descent was; how, without proper guidance and teaching, the conclusion was inevitable.

Nevertheless, our inherent nature urges us to follow our *sensus divinitatis* somewhere. So even as I was being pulled far away from Christ, abandoning the piecemeal beliefs in the God of Moses that I had picked up from my annual Easter viewing of *The Ten Commandments* and from my friend's weekly First Communion classes, I began looking for God in Eastern-inspired spirituality and the New Age.

Likewise, while discussing conversion stories with fellow Catholics, my experience is more the norm; there is rarely a watershed moment, a "Road to Damascus" event, that suddenly illuminates the mind and heart and converts anyone on the spot. Rather, conversion is a long expedition of discovery that reveals ideas and people and happenings that congeal, alongside a flood of God's grace, which finally turns one's heart to Jesus. The same is true when going in the opposite direction. Turning from faith is usually not a sudden, dramatic event, but a gradual effect of bad experiences, poor catechesis, unresolved feelings of anger or betrayal, and many other spiritually unhealthy influences.

Even for people who say they left the Catholic Church because of clerical scandals or other specific events, the true cause was likely deeper and more complicated, perhaps a misunderstanding of Catholic teachings on divorce or birth control or homosexual acts. Or maybe a bad experience in the confessional, or disgust with the perceived hypocrisy of their sinful fellow Catholics, or just a habit of convincing themselves that instead of going to church they could do some armchair-praying on Sundays and that would be sufficient.

Those excuses reveal how very important our own ordinary lives are and why it is so terribly important that we live with joy. (Is there any other way to live when we have the hope that we do?) The things that stick with us as children, how the faith is passed onto us—or not—and the impressions that are made upon us as adults all work within the heart, for better or for worse, whether we know it or not. I suspect we will not realize how all these interactions and instances come together to form our faith life and the faith life of others' until we are on the other side of this life. Let us pray that when we finally do come to know the impact our words and actions had on others, we will be rewarded with seeing our lives worked for the good, even in some very small way, pulling someone toward God and not away from him.

Of course, in any given case, there are no guarantees that we will be able to make a noticeable blip in someone's faith. Even when I could recognize good, faithful Christians around me, I thought they were an anomaly. They must just be good, gentle people anyways, I told myself, with or without a belief in Christ. Their goodness was a matter of personality, not one of faith. I often wished that I could be as innocent as they were, no longer seeking, settled in a truth that kept me content. Unfortunately, as the years went on, that wasn't to be. I didn't feel particularly innocent or naïve. In fact, I thirsted for answers to those cosmic questions that I had decided Christianity couldn't answer for me. The days of the Way Back were long gone. I went hunting, and the hunt itself became more thrilling than the answers, especially as I started to prophesy, and the dreams began to come.

CHAPTER 2

A Personal Religion: *Star Wars*, Dreams, and the Occult

I can trace many of my life choices back to a loved one's comment made in passing, or to a book lying around the house, or to a television show I once watched. And so I can say, strange as it may sound, that it was actress Raquel Welch who put me on the path to paganism.

We moved to southern California in 1987 when I was just eighteen months old, and some of my first memories are from the four years we spent there: playing hopscotch with a babysitter on the sidewalk outside our little apartment and popping Lemon Heads into my mouth as I watched my dad tinker on a car. After a lifetime in the cold Northeast, my mother began to blossom in the perpetual warmth and sunshine of San Diego and became interested in her health. White bread was swapped out for whole grain, tofu appeared on the dinner table from time to time, and we all started taking daily vitamins. Yoga and long walks became staples in her daily regimen.

At some point during those California years, the book *Raquel: The Raquel Welch Total Beauty and Fitness Program* arrived in the house. Mostly a collection of black-and-white glamor shots of Raquel from long-ago films and photo shoots, which were beautiful but a little confusing, the book also gave instructions for a complete yoga routine, which inspired me. I wanted to be like my fit mama, so when she wasn't using the book, I took it into my room and thumbed through the pages, testing my own levels of flexibility and balance.

As I got older and became aware of my body and my weight, I wanted to adopt an exercise regimen of my own. In our North Carolina home, I went in search of that old book, placed it at my bedside, and set an alarm extra early each morning so I'd have time to run through the entire routine before school. I wanted a tough workout, so I rushed through the practice, working up a sweat in my little bedroom. Eventually I could hold half-moon poses and inversions without needing the wall or a support block. I could bend over backward and easily touch my forehead to my knees in a forward bend. I wanted something harder, something more, so I added running and ate increasingly smaller portions. I became light, fast, and strong. And I was hooked.

I didn't delve deeper into yoga and its spiritual aspects until years later, but Raquel's book opened the door to yoga—and to that barnacle of New Age spirituality that drew me over the threshold.

Although that silly little book was one door in a long hallway of spiritual practices, there were many more doorways, and I was willing to open them all.

Around the time of that fateful slumber party, dreams also started playing a role in my development. These weren't run-of-the-mill dreams—the stress-induced ones, the flying ones, the I-ate-spicy-food-right-before-bed dreams. These dreams were powerful and prophetic; they revealed things to me that I firmly believed couldn't have come from anywhere but the spirit world—dreams of things that later came true in my life or in world events.

Whatever separates this world from the next thinned in my sleep, and each night I went to bed curious about what might be revealed next. Before long, I puffed myself up with self-importance. *Of course this was happening to me.* I came to believe that the Universe had chosen me to see its inner workings. I would be idiotic to ignore these opportunities to understand hidden truths. When I woke in the morning, I scribbled down as much about the dreams as I could remember, highlighting aspects that seemed especially important. Lines soon cracked the spine of my dream-interpretation paperback. I was probably the only teenager who actually wanted to go to bed early.

Sometimes the dreams were scary apocalyptic dreams filled with death and fire and bones. Those dreams were to be expected. In my New Age beliefs, the end times figured prominently. However, two of the dreams were downright demonic. Though occurring some years apart, they were connected. In the first, I was in a large shadowy cavern, lit only by torches. Awful haunting music echoed against the walls, and I watched as a well-known politician pulled out his eyeball to reveal a secret scroll kept hidden inside his skull. The scroll, when unrolled, contained the names of the damned. Though I didn't believe in it at the time, I knew I was not in a good place. This was hell.

The music struck me most, so when I heard those same out-of-tune, misshapen notes again, I knew from where it came, which terrified me. During that second time, I am convinced I wasn't entirely asleep.

I was older at that point, seventeen or eighteen, and having trouble settling my mind. Tossing and turning, I finally curled on my side, my back facing my bedroom door. Suddenly, I heard a door open heavily, slowly, on creaking hinges, and with it came that same music pouring into my bedroom. Fear filled me. Too scared to turn and see what was behind me, I pulled the sheets over my head, and shaking uncontrollably, wished it would go away. Instead, it went on for what felt like long, dreadful minutes, as if an invitation to turn and see what had entered my room. I refused. I had a natural fear that told me I didn't want anything to do with it. Then, as if the thing had gotten bored or impatient, the door slammed shut—the music gone. I never heard it again, but I would never forget it.

Had I been savvier, I would have taken that as a warning, but no, I kept chasing the dreams anyway, inviting them, wishing for them, praying to the Universe to give me more, *more*.

After my conversion, I came to learn that dream interpretations can play a legitimate role in our Christian lives. In the book of Genesis, Joseph interprets Pharaoh's dreams about the impending famine, securing him a place of honor in the royal court (and eventually bringing the Israelites to Egypt where they are saved from famine but later enslaved). God sent an angel to Joseph, the foster father of Jesus, in his dreams on four separate occasions, guiding him in his care of Mary and Jesus.

In my case, though, pursuing dream interpretation didn't bring me closer to God. I never intended it to. I was beyond the Christian God then, too self-fulfilled to fall into the constraints of an organized religion that didn't honor and promote my own path to spiritual advancement. With an insatiable hunger for special knowledge, I filled notebooks with the themes and imagery of my dreams and thoughts on what they could mean for me and for the world.

In doing so, the dreams inevitably led me to look into

non-Christian beliefs, ideas, and practices. I was exposed to the New Age western conceptualization of *chakras*, the anti-religious psychoanalysis of Sigmund Freud, and the mind-body connections of Carl Jung, which all validated my belief that I could develop, refine, and reveal my true spiritual nature—imprisoned in a crude fleshy vessel and yearning to be free—via dreams, meditation, yoga poses, and astrological signs. My spiritual journey was *personal*, so I could cherry-pick what pleased me. I could choose to believe in chakras, for example, but throw out Freud's hyper-sexualization of every mundane little thing. Bit by bit, I crafted a (barely coherent, ever-changing, always convenient) Religion of One, fueled by the narcissism from my exceptional dreams.

Had someone asked where I thought my dreams originated, I would have replied with certainty, "The Universe!" which was a synonym, along with the *Universal Mind*, the *Great Spirit*, the *Force*, etc. for the idea that all of creation—every rock, branch, sea slug, human, and spirit—was of the same substance and held the same life force, even if the thing in question was seemingly inanimate. Humans might hold a special rank among creation, but it was all to be respected together with "Brother Rock," "Sister Polar Bear," and so on.

So, although physically we see distinct forms, like people or ladybugs or buildings, the spiritual reality was that we are all made up of the same substance. If a single piece of fabric lay atop the entire world and galaxy, stretched out to each corner of the cosmos, it would push upward over mountains or dip into valleys to hint at the thing beneath it, but we would only see the fabric. My belief was that there was only the "spiritual fabric." It took the shape of various things, but in truth, there were no distinct creatures beneath it. Fundamentally, we were all the same, made of one unifying substance, though we perceived otherwise.

If we wanted to fully understand this beautiful cosmic mystery, we had to zoom in to the microscopic level and see where the tiny vibrating atoms of the table leg blended into the surrounding air, disappeared into my own leg, and so on. There, the connectedness of all creation could be seen, but these phenomena weren't something that could happen with the use of any scientific tool. No! It required an elevated mind, an awakened spirit who could see through the mundane features of the world around us, past the limitations of the tools of science, and see the universe for what it really is—a holistic creation, where everyone and everything is one and the same.

Little did I know then how this notion of oneness had elements of truth. In the Body of Christ, believers are spiritually joined through baptism. In the sense that God created everyone, yes, we are all one. All creatures ultimately find an explanation for why and how they exist in the absolutely simple eternal Being, which is God. Through mystical prayer, we may ascend to greater union with our Creator, made possible through Christ. Not all false beliefs are wrong all the way through. We are attracted to their elements of truth, and this leads us to perilous errors. Instead of rightly seeing, for example, that there must be a simple unified source of all creation, we run the risk of believing that *we* are it.

Whatever elements of truth were attracting me then, the dreams also gave me what I *wanted* to get from them—a privileged peek into a blanketed universe. I desired secret knowledge of the physical and spiritual worlds that wouldn't fade with the stars each morning; a permanent doorway to a realm that remained hidden from the eyes of the spiritually unconscious. This realm would be similar to Neil Gaiman's book *American Gods*, with its hidden world beyond the veil that gods and goddesses could slip into, and would *seem* like our world, but would be different. *Spiritual.* A place where the godlike could find peace living in a place that optimizes who they were created to be.

But how to do this? How could I extend into waking hours the quality of the feelings and information I received in dreams? How could I be sure that what I dreamed about was accurate, not cluttered by my brain processing the sights and sounds of the previous day? Finally, and perhaps most revealing about my real motivations (which were veiled under the guise of a desire for spiritual enlightenment), it was imperative that the messaging from the Universe continue. Because without such a special power, what was I? I was like everyone else.

Still a young teen, I turned to the Ouija board. At the time, I had begun a close friendship with a girl from my school who seemed like me; at least she was interested in the Universe, even if she wasn't as privileged as I was to receive as many dreams and messages from it. She was welcoming and genuine, but she was also promiscuous and was left unsupervised most of the time by a single mother who simply couldn't be home and who didn't seem to have any problems with her daughter becoming worldly at a young age. In all, friendly but a bad influence.

One afternoon, my friend pulled a Ouija board out from under her bed, and the two of us played around with it on the creaky wooden floor of her attic bedroom. We asked many questions and were amazed at the responses.

"Owen"—a friend of ours—"will die," it spelled out (and he did, ten years later, from being too inebriated to put on his CPAP mask).

The planchette then slid across the wooden board,

revealing a date just a few weeks away, the night of our upcoming dance recital at school. "Axis tilt," it said. And sure enough, around that time in the 1990s, scientists began to track a shift in the Earth's magnetic poles.

The messages we received that day were fascinating, even if we didn't know how or when or if they would come true. They certainly didn't seem fake. We were getting messages, *real* messages. Thrilled by the information we were receiving, we pressed on.

"How many spirits are here with us in the room?"

The answer came: "Seven," spelled out one letter at a time.

We were floored. To think that we were so important, so attuned to the spiritual world, that not one, not two, but *seven* spirits were reaching out to us!

I didn't realize how naïve we were until many years later, when I was deep into my Catholic conversion. We never thought to ask if these spirits were good or bad. The assumption was that surely, because our desires were born from earnest curiosity, the otherworldly beings who came to answer us would have our best interests at heart. Besides, we mistakenly believed, evil was just a construct of the human mind. Nothing that awful could persist beyond the crude physicality of this world. How foolish of us! How dangerous. The devil must have been quite pleased.

Between the dreams and the Ouija board, I began to think I was quite special, that I was privy to exclusive information. I assumed there was something different and magical about me that allowed me to slip behind the veil and see the truth that regular people, including girls who proclaimed their frightful Rapture to unsuspecting friends at slumber parties. My "special powers" went to my head.

With this newly forged confidence in my abilities

to understand the spirit realm and without any proper guidance on the subject of religion, I decided the only way forward was to create my own set of beliefs. I had been given special information, through dreams especially, but also through Ouija board messages, astrological charts, subconscious writing techniques, and the use of magical talismans. Because I had been *chosen* to receive such information, I felt sure whatever I uncovered must surely be correct. My homegrown spirituality came to rest not on a bedrock of selflessness and charity but within an ivory tower of my own making. Chin tilted at an upward angle, I fashioned for myself an idea that I was some kind of goddess, high above the rest of the dim gray world and the naïve and the foolish people in it who had no idea of what was really going on. Unsurprisingly, around this time, someone close to me accused me more than once of having a holier-than-thou attitude. "No, I don't," I retorted, even though the mean thoughts revealed a truer character: *If I did have that attitude, it would be warranted. After all, unlike you people, I've seen things. I* know *things.*

During this time, I worked hard to define my spirituality, but not just as some haphazard collection of ideas. I spent many hours researching various religious traditions and spiritual practices. I read books and articles on witchcraft, levitation, meditation, reincarnation, Native American astrology, palm reading, and on and on. Journals filled up with my attempts to pull it all together. If anyone had asked me what my beliefs were, I wouldn't have been able to name a thing, except under the umbrella term of "spirituality." Even if I couldn't name or define my beliefs in a quick elevator pitch, I knew my path and my methods were correct. Nothing could shake me from my beliefs, and there was no use trying. I had figured it out.

My pretention grew so strong that I eventually began

to roll my eyes at other spiritual seekers. Even those with enough authority to write a book on New Age practices didn't have enough knowledge to outdo *me*. Their abilities and gifts and books were merely a stepping stone that I had alighted on—and quickly stepped off—to embark on my own journey. Later, this would manifest itself as an arrogant independence and cynicism that paved the way for nihilism. My attitude stacked the tower I sat upon higher and higher, and in spiritual matters, I became increasingly dismissive and rude.

At a flea market one autumn morning when I was in my early twenties, I walked past a very large man sitting on a rather small folding chair. He rolled polished stones and little sticks in his massive hands. "Come get your fortune read! Twenty dollars! Learn the future! Avoid danger! Find love!" he promised in a southern drawl. I walked past, stopped, then backpedaled. Twenty dollars was worth it to see if he could tell me the deeper truths about myself and how far along the path of spiritual awakening I really was.

As I sat down and handed over the money, he explained what I was to do: take the little sticks and gemstones in my hands and then toss them onto the table. Barely touching them, I did what he asked.

Unhappy with the results and my apparent lack of participation, he scooped them back up and handed them to me. "Let's try that again. This time, cup them, really feel them, let them reach you."

The idea that anyone could know anything about the enigmatic me from a few crude sticks seemed ridiculous, and yet, I had paid twenty dollars. I'd play along a little bit.

Okay, I thought. *Let's see whatcha got*. After a pause, I tossed the sticks and stones on the tabletop again.

He leaned over them, studying their placement on the table. I sat back, arms crossed, silently daring him to crack through my advanced interior life to find something, anything, about who I really was.

"There's someone in your life. You need to tell them to back off. Bad energy here. You just need to tell them 'STOP.'" He held up his large palm. "STOP," he repeated.

His advice was meaningless, but rather than turn my skepticism about readings such as this toward my own spiritual beliefs, I concluded I was simply far beyond what a stranger at the flea market could manage. His method might have worked for lesser spirits, but not for someone like me.

The dreams and the Ouija board messages, on the other hand, were direct experiences of mine, not relying on anyone else to interpret them, so they became the gold standard. The Universe was willing to speak to me directly. I didn't need anyone else. In fact, I felt if I went in search of others' "expertise" in spiritual matters, I might be drawn down the wrong path. Someone who was just waking up from the illusions of this spiritually stifling physical world might need an authority for guidance, but me? No, thanks.

If I wanted to advance spiritually, I decided, I needed to collect as many experiences as possible before either I died and was reincarnated or a new age on Earth finally dawned in which the physical world was transformed and our souls were freed from their bodily prisons. At that time, the spiritual plebeians would be sent off to some kind of permanent ice-filled spirit realm or maybe their souls would be obliterated—*poof!*—while those of us who were awakened got to enjoy the new better world, perfected and free of physical constraints and ailments, until the Creator or the Universe or whatever else decided to end the whole thing and blipped us out of existence. That last part, though I wouldn't have admitted it, smacked of the Rapture that I hated, but never mind the contradictions! This vision was the future that the spirit world had revealed to me.

As I write down these memories, I'm becoming even more aware of how utterly ridiculous my beliefs were. I was suspicious of the claims of Christianity, demanding more and more proof to show that those beliefs were based on something real and not just the wishful thinking of a bunch of fear-driven men, yet I required no such validation from the New Age disciplines. Why didn't I care where I got this kind of information? Why did I think it was true? What real evidence did I have to support any of my beliefs outside of the imaginings of my own mind?

I don't think it really matters precisely *where* I got these beliefs from. A quick internet search or perusal through the New Age section of the bookstore will lead anyone to these same ideas or similar ones. I think the better question to ask is, what are the *spiritual* origins of these beliefs? For now I see that original sin—the sin of pride—and the whisperings of the devil are what get us to believe that *we* can know the truth unlike anyone else before us, as if *we* are privy to special information with a unique connection to another realm—will advance us beyond the people we are surrounded by and allow us to believe that we can become like God.

During this time, I always held the position that others could believe whatever they wanted. I had no interest in controlling anyone. Secretly, though, I didn't want *too* many people to believe in the same thing I did, because that would mean that my esoteric knowledge wasn't very special. If too many people believed in exactly the same thing I did, my New Age Club of One would lack exclusivity.

In college, I learned of a theory in anthropology, *social evolutionism*, which is quite outdated now. However, the theory gained a lot of traction in the nineteenth century, hot on the heels of Charles Darwin. This since-debunked theory held that all societies pass through the same basic levels, ranging from primitive to civilized. Take the aboriginal tribes of the Amazon, give them enough time, and they will inevitably progress to a civilized Western-like society.

I applied this theory to my beliefs on religion and spirituality. "Primitive" religions, such as Christianity, required structured hierarchy, texts, ceremonies, and concrete places of worship. Slightly more advanced religions, such as Hinduism and Buddhism, began to really get to the truth through pantheism, meditation, reincarnation, and ideas on the purpose of suffering, but still missed the mark because they too fell under the scope of "organized" religion. Finally, the most civilized of religions, the upper echelon of the spiritual hierarchy, was me . . . and others who understood that although there were truths to be found in all the world's religions, to get to the heart of our spirituality we needed to shrug off the yoke of organized religion and embrace our individuality; to think, be, and act hyper-locally (within the self), and finally unite ourselves to the Divine Within. *The Universe is God. I am the Universe. I am God.*

Can you imagine the moral implications if we were each our own god? Back then, I certainly couldn't, but believe it I did, at least in a sense. I had decided to believe that, in between each reincarnated life, we spent time in spiritual limbo interacting with others and deciding or agreeing to the major events we would endure in our next life: whom we would marry, how many children we would have, places we'd move, and so on. These decisions would also include any tragedies. So, if we went on to be murdered or raped, those events were things we had *decided upon* before our own conception. These decisions would help equalize any karmic imbalances from previous lives, as well as offer the potential for great spiritual fruits; but those fruits could only be realized if we became aware enough to accept them as such.

In the most extreme sense, then, a rapist, in carrying out his severe act of violence, might simply be on his own path to enlightenment, or he could be righting a wrong done to him by the victim against whom he is now committing the violence. Although he did something wrong according to our earthly moral standards, behind the spiritual scenes this act would be entirely acceptable; he and his victim would have agreed upon this action prior to their incarnations. Both would have the opportunity to progress, should they so choose.

As foul as this belief seems, it helped me process certain conflicts by offering an explanation as to why suffering and evil exist. They exist because through suffering we can develop spiritually in ways that we would not be able to do otherwise. Only through the Catholic faith can we understand this truth fully: "See, I refined you, but not like silver; I tested you in the furnace of affliction" (Isa. 48:10).*

This belief also enabled me to be extremely cold and unfeeling toward the suffering of my fellow man. Under my karmic belief, if a little girl was starving to death, she was starving because she either chose this method of suffering or she needed to atone for sins and failures in a previous life. Yes, most people would say this is bogus and that we should always seek to lessen suffering. But for me, I wondered why I should interfere with karmic justice. Why should I give food to the poor or water to the thirsty? Why try to save the victim of violence? To do these things might interfere with their spiritual path.

* F.J. Remler describes the necessity of suffering perfectly in his book, *Why Must I Suffer?*

It could even be a mark against me: don't we often help people because it makes us feel good about ourselves? That sounded very self-serving.

However, our intuitions and reasoning capacities rebel: this cannot be right or good.

To probe further, I wondered how the entire karmic chain got started. If people only suffer because they committed some previous wrong, then what of the first person ever to have suffered? *He* would have been wronged by undeserved suffering, in which case the karmic cycle cannot fully account for the problem of evil because it cannot explain how that cycle got started in the first place. Between these issues—moral indifference, plus a vicious unanswerable karmic regress—karma is a bad explanation for the problem of evil, superficially attractive but substantially repulsive.

If someone had posed to me any of these issues when I was a spiritual-but-not-religious believer, and had I wanted to be consistent with my beliefs, I would have had to be willing to say that rape isn't evil, or that it is not entirely the fault of the rapist because the victim *must* have played a part as well; or that the starving little girl deserved her plight for some reason we couldn't see and could never verify. I certainly would not have conceded any of that! But it logically flowed from what I professed to believe.

Now, with clarity, I can state rape *is* a serious moral evil, a heinous act of violence, and a privation of good, as is turning our back on someone who is starving and not doing what we can to offer sustenance and help. These are objective facts. We can discover these facts through our experience and our reason. An objective moral truth *does* exist. Good and Evil are real. Moral relativism is a faulty idea that I have my beliefs, you have yours, to each his own, we're all okay. I now know there is one truth.

I didn't care about being consistent. Even back then, I wasn't a full-on relativist. I did believe that we were all in the process of ascending to the ultimate higher truth—which, conveniently, was the truth that I had already figured out. As silly as it sounds to base an entire belief system on a movie, that's exactly what I did. Much of what I bought into during these years could be summed up by simply watching any of the movies from the *Star Wars* franchise.

The final of the original three *Star Wars* movies had been released two years before I was born, but with an older brother who happened to be a fan and who also kind of looked like a young Mark Hamill, the video cassettes were constantly being slipped into the VCR. I had every line memorized. As a child, I would stare in horrified fascination at the charred bodies of Uncle Owen and Aunt Ber. I winced as Luke, battered and mutilated, cried out that Darth Vader couldn't be his father. And I cooed over how cute the little Ewoks were, nearly crying every time one of them died in the final battle in *Return of the Jedi*.

The epic quest, this ultimate battle between Light and Dark, Good and Evil, ingrained itself in my very being. There *were* evil forces in the universe, and the good *must* stand up to them. In my young mind, the worst evils I knew were a bully on the school bus and a friend's overly strict parents refusing to rescind their grounding orders for a weekend slumber party. As I got older and I began to understand the deeper evil that exists in our world, the Eastern-inspired belief system that *Star Wars* offered worked for me and became the worldview I adopted for many years.

I took at face value the concept of good and evil being equal and opposite forces. Had I scratched a bit deeper and done any amount of quality thinking on the subject,

I think (at least, I hope) I would have seen how much the religious underpinnings of the *Star Wars* universe contradict one another. Though it's predicated on Christian concepts—for example, that good is *good*, that it is better than evil and so we desperately want it to prevail, which is what makes Darth Vader's final act redemptive and satisfying—but it's dressed up as Eastern spiritualism. Although the bad guys had cooler outfits and better weapons, like most people I rooted for the good guys.

And yet . . . if light and dark are equal and are destined to maintain equality, then we should see no reason to root for the good guys. If light and dark, good and evil, are two opposite and yet equal and *necessary* forces in the universe, why should we desire one over the other? Why *do* we root for the good guys, the light side of the Force?

If good and evil, light and dark sides of the Force, were equal and necessary, I—and most any other *Star Wars* fan—would not have cared if Luke defeated the emperor or if Han Solo didn't swing back around and help the rebels blast the Death Star to smithereens. But I did care; fans do care. If the sides of the Force were equal, we wouldn't care in the end who won because it wouldn't matter; but it does matter.

I was taking for granted the concept of Good without thinking through where it comes from—what defines good as good.

Had I been honest with myself or had I spent any length of time diving into these questions, I would have known that we root for the good because we *know* that evil is bad and should be opposed and avoided, and that goodness is good and should be defended and promoted.

In today's world, we hear so often people using the phrase "my truth" to convey what they think to be good and true. Their convictions about women's reproduction, recreational drug use, sexual activity, or anything else, boil down to what they perceive as true and good. And although we often disagree on what the truth is, we do agree that there is good and bad, light and dark, and that we should seek the good and the light.

The problem comes when we try to tell good and evil apart. Christians argue that it is from God that we get the best explanation for the goodness in the world (and, though it may seem odd at the outset, the only explanation for why evil exists as well). A pagan might say goodness stems from a spiritual life force; atheists might point to our species' biological desire to survive. On the opposite end, evil may be part of a balanced universe or a byproduct of our crude, animal nature.

Catholic philosophers tell us that, for something to be deemed "good," we have to look at its ultimate end, that is, its purpose, and how it best fulfills that purpose. Take a triangle, for example. A good triangle is one that has three straight sides whose angles add up to 180 degrees. Knowing what a good triangle is (what it takes for a triangle to most fully *be* a triangle), we can start describing what a bad triangle would be. Perhaps it would have shakily drawn lines, or four sides, or rounded corners. Looking at such a triangle, we would quickly know that it is a bad triangle. But first we had to know what a good, true triangle is.

Since good is the baseline, the foundation of everything, evil only shows when good is lacking. Evil is a privation, something missing from the good—a hole in a sock, a badly drawn triangle.

What could goodness be if it were missing something? And what could ultimate goodness be if it were missing *anything?* How could it not be all powerful, all knowing, all loving? Perfect good can't come in different shapes and sizes; that would mean that something was missing in each. It can't be material, bound by space or time, because then it would fade, age, get bigger or smaller, die, exist here or there, be more or less, and so on. Goodness must be changeless—so fully actualized—in itself that it can't be more purely good, any more perfectly what it is.

Though I didn't know it then, perfect good can only be God—an omniscient, omnipotent, unchanging, cosmic Fount of Being from which all goodness and truth flow.

Therefore, the truth is, yes, our universe is at war. However, it is not two independent, equal and opposite forces fighting against each other, but rather more like a rebellion, where evil rebels against the perfection of the good and thus becomes incomplete and wrong. In humanity, there are those who rebel against the good (God) and are incapable of fathoming an existence of loving servitude to him, and the good, those who have stayed or returned to God and desire to draw ever nearer to him.

As C.S. Lewis stated in *Mere Christianity:*

> Now what do we mean when we call one of them the Good Power and the other the Bad Power? . . . If 'being good' meant simply joining the side you happened to fancy, for no real reason, then good would not deserve to be called good. So we must mean that one of the two powers is actually wrong and the other actually right.
>
> But the moment you say that, you are putting into the universe a third thing in addition to the two Powers: some law or standard or rule of good which one of the powers conforms to and the other fails to conform to. But since the two powers are judged by this standard, then this standard, or the Being who made this standard, is farther back and higher up than either of them, and He will be the real God. In fact,

> what we meant by calling them good and bad turns out to be that one of them is in a right relation to the real ultimate God and the other is in a wrong relation to him.[2]

I don't intend this book to be a thorough treatment of the existence of God, how evil can exist with an all-loving God, and so on. I leave such tasks to professional philosophers. (My husband, Pat Flynn, would be an excellent resource, if I may say so!) I'm simply gesturing at a reality I think we already intuit and know and see in our world. We must ask the question: are we ready to acknowledge this reality, or will we continue to cling to the ironies and failures of an approach that may appear more sophisticated at first blush but that falls short of defining what goodness and evil are and from where (or whom) they come?

Of course, during those years, I didn't see the ironies or errors of the *Star Wars* belief system. I saw it as something profound, something that hinted at greater truths, which I, as an awakened spiritual being, could understand on a far deeper level than those who just saw the movies as entertainment.

As with many of the beliefs I flirted with in those years, I was attracted to the series on an emotional level. Anything that required deeper thinking or analytic processing I rejected as cold, unfeeling, the antithesis of the pure spiritual life I sought. I never considered that faith and reason, emotion, and logic, could be—must be—compatible because they come from the same Creator. The former trumped the latter, in stark contrast to my dismissal of the perceived failings of organized religion. I was all-in on feelings and intuitions.

However, what I thought was an enlightened, spiritual way to live was actually a path of walking death. The pain of the choices I made and the real consequences of my beliefs that hurt not only my own emotional well-being but that of the people I interacted with should have been warning enough. Unfortunately, my goal of enlightened self-awareness acted as convenient blinders when I was faced with these figurative warning signs—"Caution: Death Ahead"; "Turn back now: Needless Pain and Suffering Abound"; "Dead End." I obstinately staggered onward.

And so, into the darkest part of the forest we now turn.

CHAPTER 3

Sex, Drugs, and Abortion

My dad pulled into a McDonald's parking lot somewhere off I-95 in Georgia. We were on our way to Florida for my seventh-grade spring break, which meant a week to lay on the beach, play mini golf, eat tacos, and collect some fun stories to tell my friends when we got home.

My body ached from several hours cooped up in the backseat, so I hopped out of the car and stretched in every direction before making my way inside to the bathroom ahead of my parents. In one of the booths by the restroom doors sat three guys, a few years older than me, eating lunch. Their eyes roved over my body as I walked by them, making my skin crawl. Wanting to get back to my parents as fast as possible, I rushed through the bathroom and darted past them on the way to the family car, but I wasn't fast enough.

"Hey, baby!"

"Daaaaamn. Those legs."

"What's the rush, honey? Come here."

I stared at them in horror as I passed by and saw hungry faces. My stomach dropped. *No!* I shouted silently. *I'm not ready for this! I'm only thirteen!*

I scrambled back into the car.

"Ready to go?" My dad glanced at me in the rearview mirror.

I wanted to tell him what happened. I needed to talk through it, to process what had just happened, this thing I knew was called "catcalling" but had never experienced. I felt unclean and embarrassed. I couldn't understand why anyone would look at me and say those things. I was just a girl on vacation with her family. I remember thinking that I was too young to be treated like that. Instead, I replied, "All set."

The rest of the vacation, I got the shivers anytime I thought about what had happened, and for a long time afterward, I scanned who was sitting near the bathrooms as I walked by, wondering if that unwelcome thing would happen again. It never did, but the incident sparked something, some idea that I had now come of age, and such treatment was part of womanhood, whether I was ready for it or not. I had to accept my fate: I was growing up and decided I might as well act like it. Not long after, I began dipping my toes—and then taking the full plunge—into the waters of human sexuality.

Half a decade later, at eighteen, not only was I able to handle catcalls from boys, but I also relished the attention of the opposite sex and felt emboldened with being a young woman. However, in reality, I was still an impressionable youth without a fully developed capacity for reason, and wild with the power I felt in my own destiny. I could be anyone! I could go anywhere! Life was going to be rife with beautiful adventure!

Unfortunately, I bowed to the whims of how the mass media defined me. From the pages of magazines in grocery store checkout lines, I learned how to apply heavy makeup, squeeze into skinny jeans, and accentuate my breasts, and then I learned what to do with those looks by reading spreads such as "99 Sexy Ways to Touch Your Man." In front of the TV in my living room, I got my first lessons in sexual behavior by watching the sexual escapades played out by Samantha in *Sex and the City* and the music videos of Madonna, Jennifer Lopez, and Britney Spears from the early 2000s. Altogether, the media prepared me to engage in my own kind of licentious behavior.

To top it off, I had heard once that those who were spiritually advanced were also sexually open, which settled in my mind as a permission slip. So I let any hormone-infused passion lead the way, barely stopping to ponder if my behavior from the night before was in my best interest or maybe, just maybe, I was making the same mistakes over and over again and it was time to press pause on the trajectory of my romantic life.

I don't recall anyone acting hypersexual around me. My friends weren't pressuring me to lose my virginity. No one was calling me lame if I didn't party. Outwardly, I wasn't living in some high school coming-of-age movie from the late nineties, but I felt pressured in my own head, fueled by the promotion of sexual (and over-sexualized) behavior that I consumed through television, movies, and magazines, and paired with my own contrived spiritual superiority. So I dressed provocatively and chased boys. I loved making them want me, but as soon as I knew they could be mine, I lost interest and moved on.

Being the first in my closest circle of friends to initiate sexual intimacy, I felt a rush of power. I could make a boy pine for me, just like scenes in the movies. A boy's feelings were mine to control and became a great game to play. With practice, I perfected my wiles.

I convinced this nice Christian boy to cheat on his girlfriend when she was away on a mission trip, and with barely more than a few well-placed flirtations, I made it to the front of the line with a guy who had a bunch of my friends interested in him. I wrecked friendships and hearts, and although I, quite miraculously, didn't lose my virginity during this stage, I was doing everything possible to toe that line, spending time alone with boys whose parents were at work all day, dancing provocatively at parties, doing the very things those three teenagers in that McDonald's booth insinuated, the things that had made me sick to think about just a year or two earlier.

Within short order, my interests morphed. I watched movies with "mature" themes and paid more attention to the shows and music videos on MTV. Throughout all of this, I considered myself spiritually advanced. In order to elevate myself in the next life, my ultimate goal was to experience as many places, things, events, and to sexually experience people, as that was seen as the most intimate way to commune with someone.

In my New Age spirituality, the body was both a prison and freedom. I would use my body to get high and go on insanely long, winding runs through the forest, which would train the body to submit to my higher will, free it through the use of mind-altering drugs, and honor Mother Earth by spending time in nature. I would use my body's natural desires for sexual enjoyment with a guy to derive pleasure, as well as connect with another spirit in an intimate way and move forward in my journey. I tattooed my skin with images to show off how spiritually advanced I had become in my young life but only put the tattoos in places that someone could see if they were invited to be with me intimately, on my own terms.

My body was a fleshy prison, stopping me from being in my fully realized spiritual state, so it—and its needs and desires—was something to be tamed. My body was also the means through which I could attain enlightenment, so it needed to be used in a very utilitarian way. Finally, the body was a temple to be adorned and glorified. Spiritual practices, like meditation and yoga, were necessary to harness its power and make the outside mirror the spiritual prowess within.

A prison. A means. A temple. Surely, a body cannot be all these things, because to serve its purpose across all three categories would be problematic and impossible.

I pondered the body without any real guidance on who we are as humans, what we are made for, and without knowledge of even basic skills such as logic or rhetoric, which means my conclusions were faulty and largely contradictory. Ultimately, why did it matter what I did with my body? I wasn't as bad as *those girls,* the ones who did things with boys and flaunted it. At least I was quiet about it. Sure, I was having my fun, but I was also getting straight A's, spending Sunday mornings with my family, and still did wholesome things, like board game nights. The facade was freshly painted, but even at a young age, the structural damage had begun.

When I was fifteen, I came down with an awful case of mononucleosis, which became an answer to the age-old question of why God lets bad things happen. Sometimes we can see it in the moment, but more often it takes a look backward from far away to understand why things had to be just so. My illness kept me isolated at home for three months, thus plucking me out of my trajectory toward sin. The initial two-week sickness wrecked me and left me so weak that I couldn't even stand in the shower long enough to wash my own hair. I couldn't see my friends. I couldn't leave the house. And yet, it was a wonderful time. As summer gave way to autumn, I did nice, simple things. I sat out in the sun. I watched old movies with my mom. I read good books. I napped. All without much of the distractions of postmodern popular culture.

After hearing the news of my illness and once the threat of contagion passed, my old basketball coach came to visit and was startled to see how bright I looked. She expected someone who was worn ragged by this illness. Instead, despite the horrid fatigue, I was thriving, diverted from the dangerous path I had begun to walk down over the previous few years. This strange and lengthy bout of mono was a fortunate event, and even then I knew it. I knew there was something wrong with how I'd been living, but I also knew that I wasn't strong enough to withstand it if I went right back to life as it had once been. I wondered if maybe I could homeschool myself. I'd been doing that already to keep up with schoolwork in the months that I couldn't be in the classroom. In the end, it was decided that I should return.

I had felt renewed, better than I had the year before, despite—and perhaps because of—the illness, until I was thrown back to the outside world, high school of all places with its drama and hormones . . . The greetings I received were less than welcoming. "I thought you were dead!" "Didn't you get pregnant and drop out?" "Huh. I'd forgotten about you." I desperately wanted to retreat home, where I'd felt safe and whole for the first time in a long while, but I stayed.

In the process of readjusting to normal high school life, I wound up becoming friends with nicer kids—kids who hadn't yet been pulled into the sinful places I had finally escaped; kids who still liked to do normal, nourishing things like hiking or playing weekend pickup volleyball games. When we did sneak around, it was to slip out of the house in the early morning hours so we could grab bagels and watch the sunrise at a nearby lake.

As appreciative as I was to be in a better headspace, that goodness didn't last long. I was still too weak to head back to the basketball team after the illness, and sitting on the bench for the season, wrapping tape around the sprained ankles of my teammates led to a disinterest in that activity, which then bled out to a disinterest in most everything else. I felt adrift and ready to reinvent myself into something fantastic and new. But then September 11 happened.

In the weeks leading up to 9/11, my spiritual sense had skyrocketed. I walked around with tingling skin and a constant feeling that I needed to retch. *Something bad's going to happen*, I kept telling my mom and close friends, but how could I know what that "something bad" was going to be? When the planes crashed into those buildings, I felt certain that attack was the horror I had been sensing.

Ask people where they were on September 11, 2001, and they can tell you in minute detail, down to the flavor of Doritos they were chomping on or what song was playing on the radio, when they heard the news. I had pulled into the parking lot of a sandwich shop for an early lunch. The beautiful late summer's day felt like autumn had arrived early in the south. I was listening to Dave Matthews Band and hopped out of my Jeep to meet up with some friends, when one of them, who was notoriously sarcastic, casually mentioned a plane had crashed into the World Trade Center. Just two months before, on a visit with my family to New York, I had gone to the top of one of the towers to see my uncle's office there and take in the view.

My eyes widened. "Are you serious?"

"Yeah." My friend shrugged.

"No. ARE YOU SERIOUS?!"

He looked at me as if *I* was the crazy one. "Yes! It was on the TV in shop class."

"I've gotta go," I said and sprinted back to my car and raced home. I took the steps into the house two at a time.

"Turn on the news. Turn on the news. Turn on the news!"

My mom came running into the living room. "Why? What's going on?"

I flicked on the TV and saw, on live television, the second plane strike. I fell to my knees.

Emotionally, I didn't come up again for months. In an instant, it was as if the last bits of hope and childhood innocence I had been holding onto since the illness snapped like dry twigs. We didn't know until hours later, against all odds, my uncle had made it out of that building alive, despite nearly every one of his coworkers dying.

In the spiritual battle of good and evil, evil had made a move. In the immediate aftermath, as I prayed to the Universe for good to strike back against evil, to win this eternal war once and for all, I can't pretend I wasn't validated and feeling a little giddy at the thought that what we'd be waiting for, the End of the World, must be getting closer, and although it was a terrible loss of life and safety, at least it meant that something better would soon arrive, even if few recognized this as a sign of the things to come. So, while we holed up inside our homes, uncertain of what was coming next—a biowarfare attack, a bomb, a world war—I concluded, as I'm sure many others did during those days, that the world was ending; life could not continue after this. All my dreams, the awful retching feeling, the prophecies pointed to The End. It was just a matter of waiting as the unenlightened humans set the world on fire. Eventually we awakened folk would be living in a new and glorious spiritual reality. I began preparing myself for the culmination of this age and the start of the new—when my soul and the select few others would be free of these physical prisons and finally realize the potential of our destiny.

As much as I hoped a brighter future would arise

after this horror, in that moment, something within me snapped. I dropped to my knees on the living room floor and stared at the television, watching in real time as the hijacked plane crashed into the second building. For as much as I believed I would soon be perfected in a new spiritual reality, I fell into a depression that cost me nearly two years of my life. Witnessing the attacks on television, feeling a sort of survivor's guilt from having been in the towers a couple of months earlier on a little excursion—*How silly of me! How naïve!*—these things bloomed into a feeling of irreconcilable brokenness and led to a nosedive into anorexia that ended in yet another illness, this time more serious than the last.

I've pondered a long time over why, at certain times, God permits some level of suffering to prevent an even greater suffering and evil to occur, but regardless of why He permits it, any level of suffering can be quite catastrophic.

I refused to ask for any help in my depression as that would surely be a sign of weakness that I was not willing to share with anyone—and so the suffering was made worse by my own relentless stubbornness, internally viewed as a sort of martyrdom to the spiritual cause.

The depression I suffered manifested in anorexia, lethargy, insomnia, and an aversion to sunlight. Many days my self-imposed food rations would involve one *quarter* of a bagel for lunch and one baked chicken tender and a small salad for dinner. Fueled by my competitive spirit, I would see if I could eat just a little bit less, a little bit less, a little bit less. I told my mom, who woke up early to make me a hot breakfast, not to worry about it. I told her to sleep in; I'd take care of myself in the mornings. Unbeknownst to her, taking care of myself really meant eating a little less food each day, rationalizing that I was actually growing in virtue, in temperance, and fortitude. Who else was willing to make such a noble sacrifice? What other teenage girl was so strong? This ridiculous, self-aggrandizing mindset left no room for a larger portion of food even when I was, literally, starving. If I ate more, it would mean I wasn't strong enough to handle the pains of an empty stomach, that I hadn't tamed the flesh as a spiritually advanced person ought to have.

With little energy and with an inability to tolerate the sun in my eyes, I napped for hours every day after school, only to be awake and thinking and thinking and thinking the entire night. I looked and felt ghastly, and I was terribly lonely. Weighed down by the knowledge that I had been spiritually attuned to the impending attack on our country, and not hearing of anyone else in the aftermath who felt those same frequencies, I turned inward, and the ivory tower in which I imprisoned myself grew taller and more isolating.

I knew if the world really was ending, as I believed it was, I didn't have much time. There was so much of this world that I hadn't yet experienced. I was terrified I would miss some crucial experience that I wouldn't be able to get in the spirit realm, and so for the first time that school year, I looked around and wondered if there was anyone I could date who would help me feel less alone. I sought a more mature love.

In one of my afternoon classes, as I scrutinized each boy in the class, I finally settled on one—John, wonderfully tall, with longish black hair that curled and accentuated a strong jaw—the antithesis of my blonde and tanned self.

The old power trips I used to get from pulling boys into my orbit came rushing back with a new twist. In my mental illness, I'd become so vulnerable, so skittish and nervous, that rather than being the alluring and sexual powerhouse I envisioned myself, I became a hopeless pile of raw emotions, and it was John that pulled me into him. Though I thought I'd be the one to attract *him* and keep my cool, in reality I wrapped myself around him like a second skin and couldn't—and didn't want to—disentangle myself from him.

We became obsessed with one another, bathing in the thrill of first-time love, constantly at each other's side. I abandoned my old friends, save for my childhood best friend, and assimilated into his social circle, which happened to be the first iteration of the hipster generation in the early 2000s—coffee-drinking straight-edged waifs with jet-black hair and gauged ear piercings.

I was all over the place—hope at the end of this world, teenaged fears over my future, narcissistic loneliness at my own spiritual superiority—but this relationship centered me on one thing: my first love. He gave me purpose when I was adrift in a lack of nutrition and deepening depression. The serotonin levels kickstarted when I was with him. And thankfully, above all else, he was a virgin. He was free of drugs. He didn't drink. He was just a nice boy who played in a high school band. His love for me, that stability, kept me from the worst of myself, the girl who could have so easily retreated back to the wild and sinful place she'd been before the three months of illness and quarantine.

The obvious change in my appearance, my weight loss, my fatigue, caused great concern for my parents, but I was so irritable away from John, so undernourished and beyond grumpy, that any attempt to connect with me was met with a verbal lashing. A chasm between me and my parents quickly cracked our once rock-solid relationship. I imagine my mom and dad simply didn't know what to do with me. Perhaps they were hoping this was just a phase that would quickly pass, but still, the tension grew and the spats between us increased, as is so common in families experiencing the teenaged years.

By mid-December, my virginity was gone and I was the thinnest I've ever been.

One evening, generally annoyed by my behavior, and not feeling like cooking a meal that we would share together, my mom suggested I pick up fast food for dinner. I grabbed a burger. Despite my best attempts at controlling my appetite, I—self-controlled, steadfast me—ate the entire thing (horror of horrors!). It was the first full meal I'd eaten in months.

A few hours later, when my stomach seized up with awful pain, I thought it was because my body just wasn't used to so much food at once. I retreated into my bedroom with a bottle of Pepto Bismol, sipping on it, nearly draining the entire thing, and writhing in pain the entire night. It wasn't just the full meal that had upset my stomach; I had actually gotten food poisoning. My mother mentioned the following day that she felt a little queasy after our fast-food dinner, but for me, in my weakened state, my insides felt as if they were being ripped apart. Despite my desperate need for help, I said nothing. If I let anyone see I was suddenly in a very bad way, they might start to ask questions, find out how terrible I felt, that I wasn't just sick physically.

So although something really bad happened to me that night, it wouldn't be until after New Year's Day that I knew how bad it was.

The photos of me that Christmas, trying to smile and look normal among the glittering tree lights and shiny foil gift wrap, are just awful. The white wall behind me at our Christmas Eve dinner had a brighter color to it than my face. I couldn't walk up a flight of stairs without tunnel vision or needing to stop to catch my breath. I still wasn't eating.

One afternoon, I fainted in my bathroom, busting my lip as I fell to the linoleum. When I came to, I was finally ready to admit I needed help. I crawled to the top of the stairs and called for someone to come help me, but my voice was so tiny and I was so ashamed; no one heard. Finally, I pulled myself up to standing and decided I didn't need anyone anyways.

Looking back, I realize my guardian angel protected me, otherwise I never would have survived the suffering and confusion I felt at that point.

A few days after New Year's, the levee broke. I couldn't walk or eat. While standing in the middle of the dining room talking to my mom, I crumpled to the floor in a heap of unconsciousness. When I woke, the ambulance was already on its way.

The wait to be admitted seemed to take hours. I slipped in and out of what felt like long bouts of consciousness only to see the clock hanging on a nearby wall showing that only five or ten minutes had passed. At that point, I felt sure I was dying, and the only prayer I prayed as I floated through the darkness proved just how cavalier and selfish I was about what was happening to me, and most especially to my parents: "Please don't let me die. I haven't had enough sex yet."

Being admitted to the hospital was a saving grace. The mix of food poisoning and Pepto Bismol had ripped my intestines open and had left a scab that eventually got picked up on a scanner during one of the many tests I was subject to over my week-long hospital stay. My internal bleeding had been so intense that the emergency room doctor said he didn't know how I wasn't in a coma or dead.

During the night, I received the first blood transfusion. I could feel the blood as it pumped into my arm. Hooked up with wires and monitors and tubes, I was extremely uncomfortable, and yet I felt as if I had yet again been saved from myself. I felt an overwhelming sense of relief.

After a full week of tests (some of them truly awful), more blood transfusions, and so many arm picks that I had track marks on the soft insides of my forearm, the doctors said the bleeding had stopped and shouldn't cause me any more issues. Our trusted family physician visited me during this time. He always had a way of talking to me that made me feel like a real person, not just some kid, and though we didn't talk much about the horrible state my life was in with anorexia and depression and obsession with my boyfriend, he helped me gain a wider perspective on life and I began to heal. In fact, I ate grilled cheese after grilled cheese from the hospital nutrition cart and didn't think once about how my thinness might be slipping away. The deepest levels of anorexia had suddenly been healed, and my parents couldn't understand why I was suddenly so incredibly happy in my weak and pale state.

The relief of being plucked from my mental and physical precipice was real, though not complete. The worst of this first round of depression eased enough for me to be released, and after seven days, with nary a prayer or a thank you to any sort of divine entity or force for saving me, nor to the doctors, my parents, or even the person who brought me my grilled cheese. I remained self-centered enough to think I had done that all on our own.

With the healing from both mononucleosis and the internal bleeding, I felt an intense freedom and peace, as if God was physically pulling me out of my everyday life and saying to me, "Look! There's a better way! And it isn't the way you're trying to live. Let me show you." But, of course, I didn't see it. I had no sense of a religion or an authority. God wasn't even an option.

Feeling a bit more like my old self, my relationship with John became more fun. I was still consumed by it, still desperate, but as we inched toward summertime, the sunlight didn't hurt my eyes so much and I wasn't so lethargic. I even played basketball in a church league with some of my old high school teammates. Nevertheless, somewhere along the line, in the midst of day trips to the beach and afternoons hanging around with John and his friends at band practice, my relationship with him hit a snag. Going through his own rough patch with his parents, John withdrew from me, and we began to fight. He wanted to spend more time alone, and I suddenly found myself with nothing to do, so I wrote a lot and journaled. I participated in free association writing to get my feelings out and pass the time. As I moved toward the spiritually dangerous practice of automatic writing, I wrote and wrote, waiting for the spirit world to move me to write something that would further unlock the unseen realm and help me advance in my spirituality.

More than once during this time, John accused me of being "holier-than-thou," a nicer way of saying just how narcissistic I was when it came to my beliefs. I vehemently opposed this accusation outwardly, but inwardly, I knew that I was because, well, it was true! Who else could say they had dreams that actually meant something? Or messages from Ouija boards like I did? Who else could say they had felt the spiritual vibrations of the 9/11 attacks in the weeks leading up to it? If anyone had a reason to act more holy than other people, it certainly would be me. I was justified. I figured he was simply envious and not as advanced as I.

Fear over these growing tensions between us caused me to fight harder to stay closer to John, and if we were distanced by our own emotions and circumstances, then when we were together, we really needed to be together. Our sexual attraction for each other spread a thin blanket over the growing gap between us, like a pit camouflaged from view by a few thin tree branches.

Though I had been warned for as long as I can remember: "Be careful. You're fertile," I didn't really think it would affect me before I was ready to have a baby, so I just barely dabbled in artificial contraception, but I hated everything about condoms—the smell, the feel of them—so I had gone on the pill for a brief few weeks, gained ten pounds, and felt like a monster.

A women's health book that had been gifted to me had an interesting chapter on natural contraception, explaining ovulation and charting. It even had diagrams of how to utilize pressure points to induce a miscarriage, if need be. I couldn't abide by manmade contraception, and I had already discerned that teenage pregnancy wasn't part of my spiritual journey. Book in hand, safe and confident, I told John not to worry; I had everything under control.

I knew the day I got pregnant. Right afterward, I knew. In the bathroom, cleaning myself up, I knew, but I rationalized. Maybe it was nothing. Maybe I didn't really see the tell-tale signs of fertility that were obviously there. Too lazy to get a morning-after pill, but still concerned, I spent the following week and a half compulsively massaging the pressure points at the base of my thumb and near my ankle bone. The feeling of what was happening inside of me didn't let up.

Too embarrassed to go to the usual grocery store my family and I frequented, I went to another, where I knew no one would recognize me, and purchased a pregnancy test—a two-pack just in case—and pretended everything was business as usual as I snuck the impossibly loud plastic bag into my bathroom.

With the door locked, I peed on the stick, my hands shaking the whole time. Two lines, dark and obvious, appeared within seconds. *Seconds.*

A deep vast hole seemed to open up in my stomach and I began to sob. *Why me? Why me?* It was a litany I repeated over and over as I scrunched into the corner of the room, hugging my knees, rocking back and forth. *Why me? Why me?*

In those two words, the failings of our sex education system are so appallingly apparent. According to what is taught explicitly in school curricula and implicitly in our modern culture is this: sex has two purposes, wholly separate and distinct from one another. Sex, whether with oneself or another or more than just one other, is first and foremost for pleasure. It is an enjoyable way to connect in a unique and vulnerable way and is the pinnacle of any relationship.

Secondarily, and only when it is deemed appropriate or desired, sex can be used for the propagation of offspring. That definitely should not happen, however, until one had completed college, traveled the globe, earned a graduate degree, secured one's dream job, fallen madly in love, bought a house, gotten married (or maybe not), spent time enjoying just each other, and established financial security.

Should procreation occur when only pleasure was sought, sex becomes a failure. *You* become a failure. Or at least that's how I felt. I only went into sex for the goodness of it, not the babies. Yet here I was, starting my senior year of high school, staring up from the fetal position on my bathroom floor at a positive pregnancy test on the counter. The reality of pregnancy loomed over me. I had failed, and as I counted out the months on my fingers, I realized I would be a failure ad infinitum. The baby would come before graduation. I wouldn't even finish high school, at least not on time. I'd go from a 4.3 GPA honors student with a bright future to a tragic teen mom who would have to go to summer school and wouldn't get to travel the world or head to college.

In that moment, the world was a dark place, a tragic place. Adoption, foster care . . . I couldn't just give this baby to someone else to raise. I was responsible for it, and yet I knew that I was exceedingly selfish. Better to not be born at all than face an uncertain future or a mother who couldn't love her baby enough. And then the embarrassment of being visibly pregnant . . . people would know I failed at this whole sex thing by—of all things!—getting pregnant.

The mental gymnastics began. Once I peeled myself from the floor, I began to do my research. As far as I could tell, at roughly four weeks pregnant, the baby was simply a clump of cells, no larger than the tip of a sharpened No. 2 pencil. It wasn't human, not completely anyway, so it would be better if I got things done sooner rather than later, which the aide in the abortion clinic would affirm just two weeks later.

But the baby had something of a soul already. As I typed "Planned Parenthood abortion Raleigh, NC" into the search bar of my computer browser, I apologized to this growing clump of cells, or at least to the eternal thing that was part of it. "I'm so sorry! I just can't. It wouldn't be fair to either of us." I would say this over and over again, convincing myself that what I was doing was the best, if not the only, option.

Here, my relativism and moral weakness showed, so terribly obvious. The baby was only considered a baby if it was wanted by its parents. Otherwise, it was just a mess of unidentifiable goop. But it had a soul, something eternal, that I would be frustrating by not allowing it to be born. It was a soul that I was allowed to kill, not worth as much as I was. And yet, it was important to me that I apologized to it, got its forgiveness, and that it understood why I was choosing to keep it in the spirit world—a better, happier place than this cruel physical world. But then I reasoned that it was better for me to enjoy this life on this planet, cruel as it was, lacking in the beauty, depth, and meaning of the spirit realm—at least, that's what I convinced myself was true. I stared at the pregnancy test and the two lines. I imagined the clump of cells and saw a ruined future and a baby who would grow up with a mother who resented it. I saw nothing but disappointment and failure. I kept apologizing to it.

I'm sorry. I'm sorry. I'm sorry.

So which was it? Was the baby growing inside of me human with infinite worth and dignity? Was it only as meaningful as what I made it to be? Was it a soulless clump of cells? Or did this baby have a soul that lived on in eternity? As I apologized over and over again, begging it to understand and forgive me, and as I made the first phone call to Planned Parenthood, the answer became obvious.

What is most obvious to me now is that whatever the baby was, whether it was wanted or unwanted, whether it was a human or not, an ensouled body or not, the answer was fluid, depending on what *I* wanted it to be. The baby growth calculator online may have said that the baby was the size of a green pea and it may have had an illustration of what that baby looked like swimming in the darkness of my womb, but if I didn't want it to be a human baby, my baby, then I didn't have to think about it that way. I could choose my own definition.

My age threw a wrench in my plans to take care of this "problem." The person with whom I spoke at Planned Parenthood apologized as she informed me that in the state of North Carolina, an abortion could only be performed on a woman. At seventeen years old, I was a girl, and I either needed parental consent to receive one or I would have to go to the courthouse and prove myself competent to make the choice on my own.

Parental consent was out of the question. I was too ashamed to admit to my parents what I had done. Besides, if I was mature enough to get myself into this mess, I was mature enough to figure my way out.

I called John to my house, and we walked a little way down the street and sat on the curb.

"I'm pregnant," I growled, so disappointed in myself, so angry.

I don't remember what he said in return, but I didn't give him a chance to weigh in on what I had already planned to do. He asked if I needed money, and I practically spat, "No, it's my problem. I'll take care of it."

I refused to be fragile. I refused to be some tragic high school movie side character.

I know now that the men who hurt after abortion are not few. The guilt and shame they carry is very real. After all, the children who are being murdered are theirs too. But I gave no thought to John, except that he figured secondarily in this dilemma. He had played his part in the procreation process, but the baby in my body was in *my* body, not his. His desires to be involved in any other part of this were moot.

After he left that afternoon, news of the pregnancy delivered, I didn't see him again for several weeks, until everything had been taken care of. He pulled away. I pushed him. Neither of us made any move toward each other until afterward, and even then, that brief time apart irrevocably damaged our relationship.

I did more research, made more phone calls, and drove myself downtown to the courthouse, an imposing and ugly concrete building, where a lawyer met with me in the lobby and asked some questions about my situation, my school records, why I felt I couldn't tell my parents. Then she sat with me before a judge in a little office.

The judge was a kind woman. She asked me similar questions as the lawyer had. As I answered, I kept my hands in my lap, trembling, not because of what I was asking permission to do but because I was scared that she wouldn't give me what I wanted, and then I'd be forced to come clean to my parents. This pregnancy, after all, wasn't a blessing but a real problem, and problems like these were best taken care of quickly and discreetly.

Before she told me her answer, she looked at me with sad eyes. "You are the most mature young woman I have spoken to in a long time. I'm sorry you feel you can't speak with your parents about this, but I grant you the right to procure an abortion."

I nodded and thanked her. A sheet of paper was printed out, signed, and stamped with an official seal, and then I was back out in the autumn sunshine. As I walked across the brick road toward the side street where I'd parked my car, I called Planned Parenthood yet again, this time to make The Appointment.

Besides John, only my best friend knew I was pregnant. We never talked much about all of this again, but I remember the gray shade of her skin when I told her about it and told her what I planned to do. Her family would be away the day of The Appointment, a Saturday. She said I could let myself in and rest in her bedroom for a while before going home if I wanted.

Declining John's invitation to sit with me in the waiting room and with my best friend gone for the weekend, I made the final trip to Planned Parenthood and felt as alone as I ought to have felt. I was very small, very scared.

A heavy autumn fog clung to the air. The day was cold and damp for September. I drove out to Chapel Hill, thinking of the lyrics to the Ben Folds Five song "Brick," which detailed the singer's experience of his girlfriend supposedly going to the same abortion clinic as I was now heading. The lyrics felt very real to me and too intimate. But it didn't matter. I had convinced myself this pregnancy was simply a problem, a clump of cells, that needed to be dealt with.

I'd heard about protesters who stood outside Planned Parenthood, trying to convince girls not to have abortions, so I mentally steeled myself for that possibility, but no one was there. In fact, the entire facility seemed eerily empty. No one had told me how long the wait would be, only how long the entire procedure would last, so I wasn't prepared for the long day ahead of me. I filled out paperwork that I barely read and sat in the waiting room for a long time. Eventually, I was directed to another room, not much larger than a utility closet, lit only by dim lights under the cabinets. Eventually, the door opened but not for me. In came another girl about my age, dark skinned, with a little plastic water cup that she continually hawked spit into. She stared hard at me. The smallness inside me grew. We waited there together another hour, never speaking.

Finally, finally, I was taken from there, and it was time. The procedure was done in the usual way that these things happen, and then it was over. I was exhausted and numb.

The nurse helped me to yet another room, larger than all the others, and although I thought it had been a nearly empty building, now I saw how many girls like me were there, all lined up in bed after bed—ten of us. I noticed, too, that, besides the workers, I was the only white girl, all the others were black or Latina. I thought about my middle-class, mostly stable, good life. I thought about what their lives might be like, imagining how little we had in common, how none of us would ever be in the same room again, and the only reason we were there was this—our getting pregnant at the wrong time, in the wrong circumstances, the cramping, the bleeding, and the awful, aching sadness. I wondered where we'd go and what we'd do after we were discharged, in the coming days or weeks or years. I sipped on water and tried not to make eye contact with anyone. Some of them were chatting with each other, but it was mostly quiet. By the time it was my turn to leave, the girl who had been spitting into the cup was being brought in.

Outside, the misty rain and low gray clouds still hung in the air, but it felt colder. I felt so, so empty. I just wanted to go home and curl up and cry. Instead, I went to my friend's house, let myself in, and crawled into her bed. As tired as I was, I was bleeding heavily and restless. The loneliness felt unbearable. I called John.

He said friends were getting together later on; would I want to hang out?

Sure, I said. Being near people, being near John, felt like it should bring some comfort, but my body just felt wrong. I hadn't expected this. I had expected to feel a sense of relief, but that's not what I felt. I just felt wrong and cold and empty.

Back home, I lied to my mom about where I'd been—something about going to the movies and out shopping. I ate a little something, and then changed the maxi pad and stared at how full it was, how bright and how red the blood. I thought about telling my parents. I imagined us coming together, holding onto each other, crying together. Instead, I left without a word and went to my friend's house.

To my horror, there were people there I didn't actually know, and they thought it would be funny if we all sat around and watched a video cassette of a porn film they'd somehow gotten a hold of. *Just to see how ridiculous this is,* they explained.

And then, lights switched off, the brightness of the television screen, two young women pleasuring a red-headed man next to a pool on a sunny summer day. And there I was, sitting on the twin bed in my friend's room with a group of people I barely knew, John beside me, the bleeding and emptiness pressing against me, as I screamed and cried on the inside, hating all of it.

The next wave of depression crashed over me, the one in which I would nearly drown.

John had avoided me in the weeks prior to the abortion; now, I avoided him. Between classes at school, he would beg me to talk to him about everything that had happened.

"No, no, I don't want to. Let's just pretend it never happened."

"It doesn't work like that," he told me. I refused to give in, and he had nowhere to go but away.

It never dawned on me that a man might have feelings or opinions on an abortion. It was my body, after all, my uterus, my pregnancy, my clump of cells, my baby. John had done his part in impregnating me, but once done, he had no part in what came after. Nevertheless, he grieved too, in his own way. He pulled away from me yet again, this time in the way he acted and dressed. He started hanging out with people who were already in college, leaving me feeling like a total failure. I had long blonde hair and tanned skin and whatever clothes my mom and I had bought together. His new friends were waifs, pale, jet-black hair cut on a razor's edge. They had tattoos and listened to emotive music that unnerved me but also spoke to the scribbled mess going on inside my head. John broke up with me.

I realized afterward how much he had been holding me together in my depression and anxiety. He had kept me relatively safe from the things I might have gotten myself into, like drugs or drinking or casual sex. I was on my own for the first time in a year, trying to stand on what felt like two broken legs. John's best friend and bandmate, Taylor, held me together for a little while longer, but at the same time pulled me into his dark despairing world. He suffered greatly with depression and anxiety, self-medicating with cheap alcohol and weed smoked in his walk-in bedroom closet each night. I suffered from debilitating grief, depression, and feelings of loneliness and failure. We were a perfectly hideous match and spent hours together every day, hating our lives, finding comfort in that hatred and despair. I latched onto him. Whatever Taylor did, wherever he went, so did I. Besides, whenever we hung out, there was a chance that John might show up and I could spend some time with him, but honestly, that didn't happen very often. It was just Taylor and me and our misery.

Just as I had done a year earlier when I first noticed John in one of our shared classes, I looked around again and connected with kids I hadn't really noticed. Most of what we had in common was a desire to get high. One of these friends was Jonah, who had wild red curls and a fantastic sense of humor. Jonah was interested in classic rock, hiking, and getting high—but not the way that I had been doing it with Taylor, focused on self-hatred. Jonah liked to smoke, take long walks, talk about how to fix the world, how to tap into our true destinies and elevate our spiritual side. He liked to read about I Ching. Che Guevara was his idol. We got along famously.

With Jonah, my behavior continued on its destructive path. I still hung out with John and Taylor's emaciated emo-type of friends, but my time with Jonah was different. We talked about the future, how we were going to start a revolution in our own minds and spread it out to the rest of the world. We got stoned and unlocked hidden truths of the Universe, which just slipped out of our grasp when the high wore off. Each time we smoked weed together, it felt like we were one step closer to really closing in on something big.

Over the course of a few months, Jonah became my new best friend. Because of him, I spent more time in the fresh air and out in the sunlight than I had during my inner darkness and depression. We drove downtown and protested the Iraq War, which made us feel like we were doing something special. In the wake of 9/11, a great spiritual awakening seemed close at hand, both within ourselves and as a collective. But again and again, no matter what kind of truths we discovered in our hours-long chats about the Universe and the spirit realm, dreams and ambitions, political coups, and government overhauls, once the high wore off, we never did anything. We were all talk.

So much of the spiritual-but-not-religious life is just that—talk.

Since spiritual growth and development could only happen internally, most, if not all, that we had to do in order to advance was also internal. We weren't called to do much else. We *could* do more—meditation and unlocking a higher level of spirituality through strategic drug use, are two such examples—but it wasn't a requirement of leading a good spiritually adept life. We just had to focus on ourselves. To our detriment, this focus on oneself, while dressed up in pretty terms of flourishing, self-growth, and collective consciousness, breeds a level of hyper-independence and narcissism to the point that, though I would have denied it fiercely, I truly only cared about one person—me.

To me, spiritual life meant improved karma and the coming enlightenment that I was destined to experience. Everything I did was in order to achieve my own personal goals. If I were to champion environmental rights, it was to rack up some good karma in my spiritual ledger. If I were to protest a war or sign a petition, it was to bring about my own spiritual flourishing. The image that I had of my enlightenment—the tasks I needed to complete, the mindset I needed to cultivate in order to attain that highest level of development—was purely subjective, and so was the path to that point, including standards, guidelines of behavior, etcetera.

My truth, we'd say. Or *that's your truth,* as if truth can change depending on the person who is contemplating it. Because every person is on a different part of the path to enlightenment, even if there was some overarching Truth, everyone was somewhere on the spectrum toward it. Going back to the theory of social evolution that we touched on earlier, the Truth was that we are all on a path to enlightenment, where our souls will be freed from their earthly imprisonment, depending on the spiritual growth and work we do in each reincarnation. If we are reading this sentence in the present moment, then we haven't yet attained our highest level. Perhaps we'll get there in this life and won't need to come back here again. Or perhaps, it will take another life or two or a hundred.

So, sure, Christians may be correct because it is *their* truth that they believe in—that Jesus died for their sins. And yes, atheists who believe in nothing are also correct. They are all simply traversing along the spiritual enlightenment spectrum, probably down toward the very beginning of that line, in the cruder forms of spiritual existence. Previously, I would have put Christianity down there at the very base, and Eastern religions and New Age inching toward the most refined part of the spectrum. Again, conveniently where I was locating myself.

I had joined the mindset of an overarching truth, but that premise fails from the very start, because it asserts that there is an overarching truth—without a universal truth—and in doing so, shows that adherents to this line of thinking actually do believe there is a universal truth! Simply put, saying that there is no Truth, capital T, is asserting there is Truth with a capital T. For sure, the irony is that I was once one of them.

The "my truth/your truth" slogans are a sign of moral relativism, in which the morality we hold varies depending on time, place, culture, and even person to person, which opened the door for me. Such a pliable truth allows for all manner and matter of sins. *My* truth entailed using people to advance myself spiritually and then dumping them as soon as I felt I had derived whatever benefit from them that I had anticipated, whether friends, boyfriends, random sexual encounters, jobs, classes, or hobbies. Anything and everything.

As my weed smoking and drinking peaked, so too did my feelings of moral superiority, inflated confidence, and justification. Because I came home high so many times, when I arrived home sober one random evening for the first time in many months, I stood at the bottom of the front stoop, staring up at the door without a clue of how to walk into the house naturally. I affected what I thought was a casual persona, which was so contrary to my usual high/drunken state, my mother took one look at me and asked if I was drunk.

I still hung around with a diverse group of people—leftover friends from my days with John who were fascinated with gender-bending and sex, throwing lingerie parties where everyone showed up mostly nude and only seemed to come out at night, and new friends who laid in the sun, baking their skin and their minds. I felt free and cosmopolitan, floating between these vastly different groups, and yet miserable. I couldn't even name everyone I shared a bed with during those months. Nevertheless, I was one hundred percent convinced I was slogging through the final push toward enlightenment.

The Catechism of the Catholic Church states that "from its beginning until death, human life is surrounded by [angels'] watchful care and intercession" (366). I like to think that knowing the whole stretch of my life, how I would eventually stop running from him and let his grace get to work within me, God asked my guardian angel to try extra hard to make sure I got to the point of being baptized in his Church. I firmly believe that I wouldn't have survived this long messy journey without the constant guiding help of my angel.

One afternoon, while all my former classmates were gearing up to head to college, and I was taking a gap semester, something clicked. Just as I had once "snapped out" of anorexia, I suddenly didn't want to do anything but get well. I didn't want to suffer anymore. The martyrdom of depression and misery was exhausting. I just wanted to feel normal again.

I knew I had to make some hard decisions in order to improve my health and straighten out my life. My circle of friends were the leftovers of my relationship with John. I had only attached myself to them to try to get closer to him, hoping that we could get back together. Other friends were fun but terrible for my health. Despite months and months of smoking and drinking, of living in a fog, in the course of a day or two, I turned my back on that lifestyle and returned to my core group of friends and family who had continued to love me through all my messiness.

Goodbye to drinking, unhealthy friendships, and bad habits! Miraculously, I didn't miss any of it.

In the crisp air of an autumn day bathed in sunlight, two years after I'd fallen to my knees in front of the television as the Towers collapsed, I stood up, sober, with a happy heart that felt new and clean.

"You look like you're glowing," my mom said to me.

"I know!" Strangely enough, I kind of was.

All I'd been through had brought me to the expected outcome of my tribulation. *This is it,* I thought, *I'm finally getting close to enlightenment.*

I envisioned myself as a butterfly who had died to self in her dark chrysalis. All the pain and suffering were worth the end result, the prize of spiritual freedom and enlightenment. I was rising like the phoenix from the ashes of my life that had been burnt to cinder in the aftermath of 9/11 with anorexia and the internal bleeding and heartbreak and the abortion. *Okay, I just need to keep doing this. If I stay like this, I'll be great. I'll have made it.*

But I was doomed to fail. This peace and sense of accomplishment were completely dependent on me, and I had nothing against which to structure myself, nothing to help me navigate the tough days and the anxieties of daily life. I had no concept of consolation and desolation. I only had myself. While I was miraculously infused with newness, I had been able to make a mostly clean break from the pain and suffering; but the luster inevitably faded. I never went back to the darkness of those years, and thankfully the memories of that spiritual glow stayed with me and guided me onward. Unfortunately, I made many selfish decisions and I hurt many people as I continued on my quest for enlightenment, always working to get back to those few weeks when I felt like I was *this close* to paradise.

Eventually, even those memories began to fade, and my spiritual drive dulled until I met my husband. Exhausted and confused by the evil and suffering of the world, I let him lead me by the hand into the darkest depths: to atheism, where no divinity exists, and ultimately to nihilism, where ultimately nothing and nobody matters.

CHAPTER 4

First Comes Love, Then Comes Baby . . . and Domestic Distress

Over time, I made a considerable number of romantic mistakes, transforming myself into a serial monogamist, jumping from one relationship into the next with no more than a matter of weeks, maybe even hours, between each one, never allowing myself a chance to figure out where I was going or who I was.

This habit eventually led me four hundred miles north, to a new home in the suburbs outside of Philadelphia. I told everyone that I wanted to head out on a new adventure, when really I'd just picked up everything and upended my life for yet another guy.

Within a few months, this blissful period went from "I think I've met 'the One'" to "God (though I'm not sure there is a God) has brought me to Pennsylvania to punish me." I was working a job I hated. I was no longer dating "the One" and was instead stuck in a one-year rental agreement with my now ex-boyfriend, searching desperately for meaning.

I had fallen into an ongoing inability to take responsibility for myself. I looked to the boyfriend of the day or the dead-end job or the college courses or whatever else that had grown stale as being the root cause of all my problems. But in Pennsylvania, without any apparent outside issue to blame, I certainly wasn't about to blame myself. Instead, after years of ignoring God, I finally looked up, not so much in reverence but in search of a convenient scapegoat that would keep me from being honest about my poor choices and headstrong personality. I still refused to see my own heavy hand in my predicament. My failure was God's fault. He had done this, not me.

Nightly, I sat in a rocking chair in the front sitting room of the top-floor apartment of the Victorian home my ex and I were renting. I stared out at traffic, wondering how to get out of this deepening existential funk. I needed direction and purpose.

New Age had gone stale, and the dreams that I once enjoyed had dried up, leaving me feeling betrayed by the Universe. Why did I feel so close to enlightenment and the spirit realm, especially through my dreaming, only to have the connection to that world go dark in my sleep? What had once been a gushing flow of esoteric knowledge was now the drip-drip of a leaky faucet. I had been abandoned by the Universe. I needed to try something new.

Thinking back to my college courses on religion, I decided to try on one of the world's big religions. I had already given Buddhism and Taoism a fair shake and they weren't for me. Islam was too restrictive. Christianity a nonstarter. That left Judaism. And the more I looked into it, the more plausible it seemed for me. Here was the God of the Universe that I craved but without the middleman of Christ. Here was ancient ritual and meaning without having to go to a boring Christian church service. Here was a sensical and simple way of life: the Ten Commandments.

I dove into books about Judaism. What did the religion espouse? What historical basis did it have? What did I need to do to practice it? I read books about how God could be found in nature in the present day, just as He had revealed himself to his chosen people millennia ago in the desert, on the mountaintop. There wasn't a need for a church. Just go into the woods and find God.

In September, during Rosh Hashanah, I drove to Valley Forge National Park, scrambled down the rocky ledge to the bank of one of the streams that runs through George Washington's old encampment, and scattered breadcrumbs on the surface of the water, envisioning my many sins drifting away from me with the current. I wanted to feel free from them; to show God I didn't want to carry the burden of them anymore. I went home and made a honey apple cake and ate fish to celebrate my first Jewish holiday, and then spent it alone, clueless as to what I was really doing.

My ignorance was overshadowed by another more glaring one—I didn't believe any of it.

What I had hoped would be transformative was actually quite anticlimactic, a repeat of what I had experienced every fall in recent years. Crazy. Restless. Yearning for spiritual growth. I thought the veil was being pulled back again, and I was glimpsing something of the spirit and the divine. In feeling weirdly stretched between this world and the next, I thought God was calling me to continue to explore the invisible. I've since come to know that my heightened anxiety and distended awareness each fall was more likely to be post-traumatic stress from my first brush with depression in the wake of 9/11, not the spirit world trying to communicate with me. However, I didn't know that then, and I spent the entire fall, as I had for the previous seven years, journaling furiously, begging God to save me, and wondering if I was on the cusp of enlightenment or salvation or the end of the world.

By the time the last of the leaves fell from the trees, I was exhausted and hollow and, having felt nothing spectacular, abandoned Judaism.

After a few months' break, I decided to start dating again. If nothing else, that would lift my spirits.

I soon met a guy at the gym where I worked out every day on my way home from work. This fellow, quite a bit older than me and stable, had roots and good family ties and his own house. He was everything I was not. I had a few hangups. He was, of all things, *Catholic*, which was a struggle for me. Nevertheless, during the course of our relationship, I did go to church with him a couple of Sundays. I tried to imagine myself a pious little Catholic girl, sitting, standing, kneeling in the pews, following along, but panic seeped in. That wasn't who I was. I was all wings, no roots. I was wild and free and untamable. His vanilla life was structured—soft pretzels and cold beer every Sunday during football season, Friday evenings at home, and watching our shows together on Wednesdays. Chores on Saturday mornings, dates on Saturday nights. It was all so scripted, so banal. Was this what it meant to be a Christian? If so, it was so *boring.*

While my boyfriend remained unaware of my growing restlessness, I began to look for ways to channel it. At first, I took my entrance exams for graduate school and began filling out applications to various schools around the country. If nothing else, I figured I could use the bachelor's degree I'd received in Cultural Anthropology as a springboard for a master's and eventually a PhD. I could live the academic life, free from these everyday struggles of the outside world, safe in my collegiate life.

Nevertheless, I kept hesitating on submitting the

applications. I didn't really want to go back to school, didn't want the debt, but I felt insufficient working my desk job, dating this vanilla man. A few letters after my name might change that. Still, I hesitated.

I picked up a second job, checking people in at a tanning salon owned by an acquaintance, and told anyone who would listen about my existential confusion.

On the days I drove to my boyfriend's house after either my primary job or the secondary one, heading into his very set routine, I began to feel a gripping panic in my stomach. *No*, I would say, fighting against the rising tide of anxiety. *No, his life is a nice life. I can handle this. It's good for me. I can get used to this. If things just stay exactly as they are now, I can hold on.*

A tanning salon coworker, fed up with my complaints about my life, suggested that rather than just bemoaning my current situation, I should actually do something—anything—until I made a concrete decision about my future. As she made this declaration, I looked down at that month's edition of a local newspaper in my hand. An idea hit.

All right, I figured. *I'll go back to writing. I always liked that.*

In a brief email, I pitched the local editor proposing to fill a gap I'd noticed in his paper: with a column on fitness or wellness. He brought me on for $50 an article, and I began scouting the local fitness scene for stories to write. I reminisced about playing basketball with my dad; I advised on healthy ways to celebrate the holidays; I gave insights into easy ways to get moving and not be so sedentary . . . but in a matter of months, I was running out of ideas. I had to tie each of my articles to someplace local, but our small college town had lots in the way of funky bars and restaurants, not so much in the way of healthy living.

During one of my brainstorming sessions, I thought of Laura, a woman I used to work with. She'd had a huge physical transformation, shedding a hundred pounds or more, and kept it off. I refused to believe that she was anything but the super-fit coworker who could do an insane number of pull-ups until she pulled a photo of "the old me" from the folds of her wallet, and sure enough, she was telling the truth. And she was, no doubt, one tough, hardworking woman. Not long after, she quit office life and went to work full-time as a kettlebell instructor at the gym where this amazing transformation had occurred. It just so happened that Dragon Gym was right on the border of the town, within the acceptable mileage to be spotlighted in an article for the newspaper.

I called the gym and made an appointment to do a kettlebell class one evening after work the following week, hoping that Laura would be my teacher, feeling good about myself for taking that initiative. But as the day arrived, I found myself lethargic and wanting to flake on the class. Who really cared if I was a no-show? I had other things to do. I was tired, and I had a long commute back home. I decided I'd think of an easier article to write before the deadline.

Despite my litany of excuses, I drove to the gym and saw Laura's old beat-up gray Saturn in the parking lot and decided that I would feel bad if I flaked on her. I walked into Dragon Gym, only to find out that it wasn't Laura's car outside, rather it belonged to another trainer at the gym, who, besides oddly having the same car, also happened to be in charge of the kettlebell program. Although he wasn't my teacher that night, once the class I had signed up for was over (and I was a sweaty mess), he sat me down to talk about kettlebells and my article for the paper.

He introduced himself as Pat and told me that if I'd

like to write another article about Dragon Gym or kettlebells or, heck, even just one on himself—how humble—I could. I politely declined. "I'm more of a columnist," I explained, "and don't really write pieces like that."

"I'll give you free kettlebell training."

That got my attention. Personal training can be a major investment, and my bank account was definitely not overflowing. In this trade scenario, it seemed as though I was getting the better end of the deal. "Okay," I said, "for free training."

We met at a pub later that week for the interview, and we had such a fun time together and I felt such a strong connection, the interview went in the totally wrong direction. Suddenly, *I* was pouring my heart out to *him*! I told him practically everything, from the abortion to my fears of mediocrity and mortality and everything in between. So, we scheduled another meet up . . . and another. And pretty soon, I was writing a detailed pros-and-cons list about whether I should stay with my boyfriend or be with Pat, and I was placing my phone face down on the counter at my boyfriend's house in case Pat texted me something that I didn't want anyone else to see. He also stopped by the tanning salon on the nights I worked and took me out to lunch during office hours.

Despite having been upfront that I had a boyfriend—a very serious boyfriend—Pat kept insisting on seeing me. So, we had beers together, took walks, and watched TV. Just nice friendly things, but something more was definitely happening beneath the surface. Pat was the exact opposite of the man I was dating. He was fifteen years younger than my current beau, vivacious, adventurous, and made me laugh. Even though we started out strictly as friends, I yearned to be with him every minute of the day. If there was actually a thing such as soulmates, I felt sure he was mine.

While sitting in a coffee shop one afternoon, he pulled up a summary of our astrological compatibility on his laptop just for fun. The validity of astrology had grown on me through the years, as meaningful dreams had ceased. I would often consult the stars for ideas on jobs, romance, travel, and projects. I wasn't silly enough to believe that this was infallible knowledge or even that it was the best cosmic information, but I felt that it at least pointed in the right direction. A horoscope may not provide specifics, but it might get enough right to make sure I was staying on my spiritual path and not veering off into the weeds of unnecessary suffering and confusion.

As Pat and I read through our compatibility chart together, the little hairs on my neck and arms stood up. But more than that, I felt as if we were being joined together, as if some cosmic union took place as we read the words aloud.

"Did something just happen?" I asked him.

"I think so," he said, and we stared at each other for a long time.

I had sworn off feelings, sworn off jumping headfirst into another ooey-gooey relationship, but here I was, feeling as though my soul was being joined to another over coffee in a strange and seemingly spiritual event. Did the astrological compatibility chart know something we didn't? Was our growing relationship—our destiny to be together—written in the far-off starry landscape? Was this the spirit world telling us we'd found our soulmates?

It was an attractive idea, and I permitted astrology some credibility, although I felt much too sophisticated to believe the stars were actually divine entities or ruled by ancient gods. However, if there was knowledge kept in their movements—and I felt sure that there was some—then I, as an enlightened soul, could certainly access the secrets held in the stars. Now looking back, my hunting for knowledge and truth in celestial bodies seems a misguided attempt to find answers to questions that only God knows—answers that he gives and only on his time.

In consulting the astrological signs, I recommitted the original sin of pride—that *I* can know everything. That *I* can unearth ancient and eternal secrets through *my* own abilities, completely apart from God—and as with every sin, it depleted my soul of true life, the very thing that I, a seeker, was trying to avoid. Here in my desire to see my destiny, outside of the bounds of the relationship that God has asked me to have with him, I ushered into my soul the death of his grace, thus destroying the relationship with the One who deeply and dearly desires to embrace each of us in everlasting love.

Without knowing any of this, and still thinking there was something to the study of astrology (beyond the perversion of a reliable scientific study), I felt joined to Pat in an astonishing way. Although there had been quite a few loves before him, this was altogether something new and wonderful. I had walked out of ordinary life with its football Sundays and nine-to-five office jobs and into this wild, wonderful adventure with Pat. My mind was made up. I didn't need any more pros-and-cons lists or meditations. Within the week and for the final time in my life, I disappeared from a relationship. With barely a word, I said a brief goodbye to my boyfriend and happily agreed to belong to Pat.

Our time together was perfect and fun and so deliciously sinful, though neither of us would have ever used that word at the time. We were in love, and it was amazing.

But as heavenly as our relationship felt from the start, reality was a bit different. We both carried baggage from old relationships, and in a particularly hurtful way, some of Pat's exes did not always stay in the past, sometimes reemerging at unexpected and vulnerable times. So, despite a wonderful beginning, wounds and scars had begun to show. Because historically I had abandoned relationships before I could ever get hurt, I never learned true forgiveness.

My ex tried to get in touch with me to find out why I ended such a good thing. I didn't have the heart to tell him the truth—that I had met someone infinitely better suited for me, so I danced around his questions and finally said I couldn't be with him any longer because of two main factors: he was so set in his life, and he was Catholic. I could never really be with someone who was like him, including someone of his faith.

Within days, everything about my life changed. Pat and I rarely spent a day—or night—apart. I skipped out on work early, came in late, took long lunches. I went to every one of his kettlebell classes that he taught at the college or the YMCA or the gym. As a joke, Pat snuck me into one of his accounting classes one afternoon, where the professor spent the entire session eyeing me suspiciously. All the love I was willing to pour into Pat, he, amazingly, was willing to give back in his way too. He sent texts to me constantly when we were apart. He'd swing by my office and have me come straight over to his house after work was done. He'd buy me little gifts and take me out to dinner and for drinks nearly every night. We hit golf balls off his roof at night, took long drives to look at the stars, danced in bars, sang karaoke. Our time together was perfect and fun and so deliciously sinful, though neither of us would have ever used that word at the time.

Several months later, however, I discovered that Pat had still been talking with two ex-girlfriends. His texts and emails to them were far different than the fawning love letters they sent to him, conveying clearly that he had made a break from them, but the situation still seemed elastic and malleable. The perfection I thought had existed between us for four months was shattered. *I* had made a clean break with my past and *he* hadn't. I had given my entire self for him, and yet, despite appearances, he hadn't done the same.

I sat on this knowledge for a day or two, then finally confronted him as we sat in my Jeep while parked behind our apartment. I had never, since Mike and the abortion, loved someone like Pat, and never had I let anyone get so close to my heart. In ten years, I hadn't been dumped or rejected, and yet here, when I gave myself completely to another for the first time in a decade, I felt utterly rejected and soiled and devastated. I had placed all my hopes and happiness in Pat, and he devastated me.

Fortunately, something miraculous happened. I told Pat how angry I was, how betrayed and devastated he made me feel, but I didn't kick him out. His eyes said he fully expected me to, and I had fully intended to, but something stopped me. Something said to me, *Wait! You and Pat aren't through yet.* And despite all my past experiences, all my plans, all my rage, I listened, and I told Pat I wasn't going to break up with him. I told him I'd forgive him.

Unfortunately, the brokenness and the anger and the pain didn't heal properly. The scarring was obvious. Despite saying I would forgive him, I didn't. I couldn't forgive. I knew nothing about forgiveness—how to receive it, how to give it, why it was so critical in the first place. I had never stuck around long enough to be in such a situation.

Often, in my dreams, whenever badness started to creep in, my brain's default reaction was to run and hide. I didn't have a fight response, even on a subconscious level, and forgiveness requires a fight response.

Forgiving someone who has caused deep emotional pain requires recognizing that the person and the relationship are worth the effort it takes to reach forgiveness. In all of my spiritual journeying, however, this was an alien concept, and a very uncomfortable one because the root of forgiveness and, hopefully, ultimately, reconciliation is a deep, abiding humility that arrogant, spiritual me had no interest in cultivating.

If someone hurt me, my only response was to run.

So although I would say to Pat, "I forgive you," I had no concept of how to actually go about doing that. I could pretend to the best of my ability, but my false pretense created a thin veneer, as if a sheet had been thrown over a pile of bricks, and we called that a finished house. Instead, the wounds set the foundation for a crooked, misshapen home that nothing in this world seemed able to fix.

I subtly withdrew in some ways as the inevitable hurts of our relationship stacked up, yet in other ways I became more desperate for Pat's attention. For the first time in our brief relationship, the playful bickering and occasional verbal jousts turned into arguments and downright fights. Despite my stubbornness, we loved each other and there was still a lot of good about us being together, but Pat was becoming weary chasing after my forgiveness.

A year into our relationship, we had a pregnancy scare, and for the first time, we seriously talked about what we'd do if I was pregnant. We were living together full-time. Pat had moved into my apartment, and with my well-paying office gig, I was supporting him as he grew his fitness business. We talked about marriage, too.

The thought of going through another abortion, those awful memories, rose like bile. I had chosen death. At that time, it had made sense to do so—I was seventeen and not even a high school graduate. But how could I justify abortion in my late twenties, with a good job, and a man whom I loved? I knew I couldn't, but what if Pat, who was four-and-a-half years younger than me, didn't want the baby as I did? What if he wanted to enjoy more of his twenties without the burdens of fatherhood? What if he wanted me to have an abortion? Was I brave enough to be a single mother? What would my parents say? What would people think?

But Pat, despite his age and immaturity, said something to me that I could not have anticipated:

"Babies are always a blessing."

I was taken aback. "They are?"

He nodded and smiled. "They are."

No one had ever said that to me, least of all some college guy. Babies were burdens, things that kept you from fulfilling your lifelong dreams. They were things that responsible grownups had, people who were wise and stable enough and could financially and emotionally support a little life. Babies were for after you'd lived a life as a "D.I.N.K." (Double Income, No Kids) for a while. They were not blessings but concessions, and parenthood was just another box to check in the laundry list of life's expectations. High school—check. College—check. Find the perfect job—check. Travel the world—check. Find your soulmate—check. Buy a house—check. Save up a year's worth of income—check. Have a baby.

Anyone who did that out of order was to be pitied because they were giving up by not hitting all those other milestones before being weighed down by parenthood.

Relief and comfort and love flooded me. I didn't need to get another abortion. We could keep this baby and we could keep loving each other, even in our imperfect ways. For the first time, since the abortion a decade prior, a part of me that I didn't even realize needed healing began to heal.

But then, there was no baby. I wasn't pregnant. Instead of being relieved, I was surprisingly (at least to me) sad. I loved Pat so much that I realized I wanted a baby; I wanted *his* baby. I wanted a family with him.

I confessed to a friend that I would be happy to be pregnant. I was twenty-seven, in a relationship with someone I cared for deeply, and living a life that looked like marriage. Despite our troubles, I wanted everything about Pat, including his child, in such a way that felt almost like some kind of biological survival mechanism.

Unfortunately, while I was coming to this realization, Pat was facing his own demons.

For as long as he could remember, he suffered from generalized anxiety, brought on by various tragedies and traumas of a somewhat unstable childhood. He decided he didn't want to continue popping a pill every morning to calm his nerves. He woke up one day and said, "I'm going to write a book. Oh, and I'm getting off the meds."

Having no personal experience with anxiety or mental health medications, I didn't think twice about his decision. I just shrugged and figured he knew what he was doing.

In the daytime, he poured his attention and energy into writing his first book. At night, crippling anxiety and insomnia set in. Sleeping in our bed together made him stress about trying—and failing—to fall asleep, so he slept on the couch in the living room, but I hated that. I wanted to be with the man I loved, so I started sleeping on the couch with him. But the TV also had to be on, otherwise, how could he calm the noises in his head if there wasn't noise outside of it? So we watched nice, enjoyable things, but once he found something that really put him to sleep, it was hard for him to watch anything else. I can't even count how many times we watched *The Fantastic Mr. Fox*.

I felt great turmoil watching him—so strong, confident, hardworking, and attractive—turn into mush every night. As the months wore on, he became increasingly unable to leave the house without me or some other trusted person along with him. Our texts stopped being so cutesy and fun and became more panicked and needy. "Are you there?" "You're there, right?" "K, going out. You'll be by your phone?"

I did research and knew that since he chose to get off the medication cold turkey without any guidance, he was doing something that wasn't at all advised and there were sure to be consequences. I knew I was a crutch, but I also knew that Pat's anxiety wasn't Pat. Besides, after the wounds inflicted earlier in our relationship, wasn't it better to be needed than not? I loved him, and I wasn't going anywhere, even if his insomnia, anxiety, and agoraphobia were worsening. I didn't always recognize him as the same person I'd met in the gym that night not so terribly long ago.

A few weeks later, we went on a cruise to the Bahamas with Pat's family, escaping the frigid Northeast winter, and I took a pregnancy test along with me. I had a gut feeling. I also felt like I had a million weird symptoms at once and had plugged them all into the WebMD symptom checker before we left town. The website spat back that either I was pregnant or had cat scratch fever or cancer or a hodgepodge of other illnesses. The pregnancy test confirmed what I already felt.

Despite his ongoing discomfort, I approached him with a grin. He looked at me suspiciously, but nothing could dismiss my elation. The thing that I had been hoping for—but at the same time afraid to hope for—was happening. We were going to have a baby. We had an awkward celebration in that tiny cabin on the cruise ship. In my already wildly fluctuating hormones, I felt two emotions beginning to bubble up: joy and hope. Joy that I was going to be a mom, and this man and I were carving out a beautiful little life together, and also hope that, even though I knew nothing about motherhood and despite our rockiness, everything would be okay.

My tentative excitement buoyed me, but the next few months were *hard*—a whirlwind of throwing up, mood swings, fights with Pat, nerves over telling my family, trying to figure out baby gear and names. I looked forward to giving birth but had no idea what motherhood was like. I was one of the youngest people in my family and had only been around babies briefly, usually when a cousin visited with one of theirs. I loved my dog, and so very stoically concluded that I would probably love my child in a similar way.

I also began to imagine what I would be like as a mother, the image of which was a complete fabrication, mostly shaped by celebrity maternity photo shoots in magazines. "Goddess" was one word that repeatedly came to mind. I would be fertile—a beautiful, shapely woman who was this baby's own little land of milk and honey. I would be sexual—a beautiful, shapely, adoring woman for her man. I would glow and tend to my home as a true queen of the natural order. I had big plans for my womanhood. I wouldn't "let myself go." I would bounce right back to my fit pre-baby body. I would look and feel fabulous, an enviable blend of sexuality and comfort. The pregnancy was all about *me*.

As any seasoned parent could predict, my daydreams did not line up with reality, which came as a striking blow in October of 2013.

After many hours of labor, which wasn't at all what I'd envisioned, the doctor guided my hands and placed them on my baby's shoulders. "Here. You deliver him."

My grip tightened on impossibly tiny shoulders, and

with the doctor's help, I guided my son out of my womb and into my arms. As I laid eyes on him for the first time in flesh and color, versus the grainy two-dimensional ultrasound images, light flashed through the room. Words zipped through my mind faster than my son could unleash his first beautiful cry: *I will kill for you.*

The overpowering love intensified the longer I stared at him, which was not at all what I had expected. This emotion was not the fun, cutesy puppy love of dog and owner. This new love was intense and all-consuming. This little boy was mine, and I was his mother bear. I was hopelessly in love, and those initial glimmers of joy and hope were now exploding fireworks—an unending grand finale. The ideas of who I would be as a mother shattered and new ones formed, all within the first three minutes of clutching my baby to my breast. The world no longer revolved around me or Pat or even the sun, but around my son.

Pat, however, did not immediately become the father to my level of mother. He was scared to hold Roan, even sitting down in the armchair next to my hospital bed. He handed him back to me within just a few minutes. I knew it was partly his anxiety that made him feel insecure, but I wanted him to snap out of it. Why wasn't he immediately consumed with love for our son as I was?

For all the talk about babies being blessings, Pat flitted in and out of fatherhood, focusing on the growth of his business, his next book, his bank statement, his next car. He was chasing happiness in the world, while I was holding happiness in my arms and nursing him and rocking him to sleep.

I discovered true happiness is neither of those things, and we grew further apart from one another, and a little bit more miserable with ourselves as time went on.

My images of motherhood continued to falter when

I struggled mightily with breastfeeding. With a high pain tolerance and no idea of what I was doing, I let Roan foster a poor latch, which caused horrific damage to my body in a matter of weeks. At a checkup, feverish with mastitis and infection, even my doctor shook his head. "It's bad." Every time Roan nursed, I cried in pain and he had blood from my breasts in his spitup. I couldn't wear a shirt for long because the scabs would stick to the fabric, which caused me more pain and crying as I peeled it away. Nevertheless, I was stubborn and refused to give up. For as much as I had ideas about Christine as Mother, and as much as many of those ideas were obliterated by actual motherhood, I was unwilling to give up on breastfeeding.

At the same time, something seemingly insane happened to me—I didn't want to go back to work. I didn't want to leave my baby. I couldn't bear to have him away from my arms. I thought women could have it all—a career and motherhood, a great bank account and a happy home life—but as it turned out, *I* only wanted two of those things, and neither had anything to do with being away from my child for eight-plus hours Monday to Friday.

The breaking down of this lie that we can do it all/have it all broke me further. Anxiety flooded through me at the thought of packing up and going back to the office after just twelve weeks at home with him. I needed more time—to get my body able to wear clothes, much less fit into the pre-pregnancy ones. I needed more time to get Roan on a good feeding/sleeping schedule, time to figure out childcare, because with the hospital bills, becoming first-time homeowners, the cost of furnishing said house, and the myriad other bills we were accumulating, we couldn't afford daycare.

More strenuous was the realization that there surely was no person on the entire planet I could trust with my precious baby. Petrified of this fleeting time together, I clung to Roan ever tighter and continued to push Pat away.

Did I have postpartum depression and anxiety? Possibly. At the very least, the stress, fluctuating hormones, breastfeeding trauma, home buying and moving, Pat's continued work on his books, inability to find childcare, pressure to maintain a quality relationship with my husband—these things not only piled on top of me, but felt compressed against me, as if I was at the very bottom of the heaps of garbage destined for the trash compactor.

There were blessings in the suffering. My managers back in the office were caring and understanding enough to let me work from home for a few extra months while my body healed, and during that time, one of Pat's closest friends from college who couldn't find a teaching job in time for the following school year, agreed to watch Roan a few days a week for a very reasonable price. My mother-in-law and Pat were able to cover another day, and then I was able to work from home one day a week. So, the day my son turned six months old, I walked back into the office, miserable but not nearly as panicked as I would have been at the twelve-week mark.

Still, the struggle to be away from Roan for even a day was intense. How could it be, I wondered, that I wasn't happy to be back at work, creating PowerPoint presentations and wearing cute outfits and makeup for thirty-five hours a week, surrounded by office friends and cups of coffee that didn't grow cold in the wake of diaper changing and laundry folding? At work, I was making money, paying off college debts. Pat, Roan, and I were taking fun vacations, looking like cool, put-together parents with our little guy in tow on airplanes. Wasn't this happiness? Or at least this was the happiness that "society" promises because I seemingly had it all. We were living the millennial "adulting" dream: two incomes, a chubby little baby, two new cars in the driveway, fancy dinners at upscale restaurants, and homeownership. We were doing it all without those pesky old-fashioned ideas of stay-at-home motherhood or even marriage.

I was miserable.

Pat wouldn't marry me, at least not at first. I didn't want to be away from my son. I was more than happy to give up the vacations, cars, dinners, and go down to one income just so I could be at home where I increasingly felt I belonged. I wanted to be married and I wanted to be a homemaker, but Pat wasn't interested in any of that. Those things might take his focus away from making money, growing his business, leveling up what car he drove.

Eventually, I somehow miraculously finagled an engagement ring and a wedding. We had already planned a fun trip to California's wine country with friends, and since we were already spending the money, I convinced him to have the wedding while we were there. Anyone who wanted to attend could join us.

Pat agreed!

With a friend officiating in front of fifteen or so family and friends and our eleven-month-old son, we made our vows to one another.

We were husband and wife!

But were we really? Like on a deep, spiritual level? No, I can't say we were. I refused to drop my maiden name, instead opting to hyphenate it. God forbid anyone think I wasn't my own woman and would dare to take a man's last name! We actively avoided pregnancy. We both looked to pornography as a stand-in when the other person wasn't emotionally or physically available.

I can't say that we were *completely* unhappy. Despite our problems, we did have a lot of fun together. We went on dates, we threw parties, but more often than not, there was some barrier between us—other people or food and drink or movies or some distraction to buffer the tensions and distance between us.

And there certainly were still tensions. Owning his own company, Pat liked the security of my job, income, and stellar health insurance, all things he didn't have guaranteed with his work. I was also trying to find happiness and comfort in the hours after Roan's bedtime, so I drank a lot of wine in the evenings, which made me physically withholding instead of loose and fun, as it had in my youth. Pat was sexually frustrated, and I was angry at him for even asking me to join him in the bedroom. How could he want *that* when we were in the thick of taking care of our son and there was a love there, between parent and child, that I had never experienced before—something spiritual and deeper than any kind of "crude" sexual love.

My understanding of womanhood, manhood, parenthood, sexuality, and marriage were so faulty, so messy, that only by God's grace did we ever arrive at healing and understanding. My conceptions of myself as woman, as wife, and as a mother were deeply disordered, and so it comes as no surprise that my expectations of how Pat and I were to relate to one another were as well.

On the one hand, I was holding on to the secular notions of womanhood: I was stronger than any man. I didn't need a man. I shouldn't want to be at home with my child, but rather in the workplace where my real talents could be best utilized, not wasted in quiet, ordinary domestic life. My prowess lay in my physical beauty, mental sharpness, and my achievements in the public eye.

On the other hand, I held on to my New Age understanding of the body and soul. That our physical body is a crude outer shell, a prison for our elevated spiritual selves, which are constantly trying to break free. So, in my mind, the physical body was either something to use (or abuse) as a tool, but ultimately, we aspire to something higher than what we can see and feel and experience around us.

Contrary to those beliefs, the love I felt for my baby boy transcended any of the physical love I had come to know and had perpetually misused in relationship after relationship, including this one with Pat. Now that I had experienced this wonderful spiritual love, true love seemed completely incongruous to the crude, physical stuff. I could barely even bother to care for anything of this physical world—Pat, the workplace, my own physical health. My child was my joy and hope that there was meaning and purpose to my life. I clung to him.

More than once, I threatened to take Roan and leave. Maybe go to my parents? I don't know. I spouted off empty threats, but Pat grew weary of hearing them. He was typically quick to forgive, but forgiveness was coming later and slower and felt incomplete. We fought more and more, mostly because I was picking fights and he was taking the bait. If we fought, at least we were talking to one another, which was better than the silence separating us, better than staring at the top of the other person's head while they scrolled mindlessly through social media or watched YouTube videos or whatever distraction captivated us at the moment.

We hit a critical point one night when it was Pat, not me, who packed a bag. Halfway down the stairs, I stood, baby in arms, shouting after him. He looked up at me. The glare from the overbright hall light made his face look angry and yellow, unhealthy and mean. "Unless you apologize and are ready to move past this, I'm leaving. I'm really leaving, Christine."

"To where?"

"I don't know."

Whatever our fight was about—and I guarantee it wasn't about anything in particular except my desire to fight—was it worth breaking up our home? I didn't want to be a single mother of one. I wanted a complete family and home life. I wavered in stubborn pride, but with great effort, I said, "Wait."

He stopped, looking at me expectantly.

"I'm..." I could stop now and my ego wouldn't take the hit, but no, the word was coming out before I could think more about it. "*Sorry*."

I felt as if I'd been socked in the gut. Nothing was worse than apologizing. But amazingly, Pat carried his bag back upstairs and stayed. The apology saved us.

There was a cost, however. My concept of self-worth was tied almost exclusively to my pride. I had nothing else to believe in but myself. There was no higher power to rest in. I had no concept of being a "beloved daughter of God." I just had myself. If I was a pushover, if I let Pat get away with things that irked me or downright offended me, who was I? A doormat? What did that say about me? That I had no self-respect?

The more I pondered what I was, who I was, the more I became aware of my inadequacy. I was a mother of one, now pregnant with another, who unwillingly worked in an office to fulfill a dream I was told I should have, paying off college debt for an unproductive degree and a nice car. The only really truly bright spot at all was my son, but everything else about me felt cynical, stagnant, and unworthy. The worst part was the thoughts of my mortality. In one hundred years, we'd be dead and dust. All this time and love and attention and care I put into raising him would be for nothing, which terrified me. My absurd perspective sent me spiraling downward at an increasing rate.

Finally, one brief conversation that my husband and I

had one afternoon left an indelible mark on my psyche. I let myself slip down to rock bottom, where everything I ever wanted to believe about my value and uniqueness as a person, and everything I had believed about my spiritual journey, sank into the yucky, sticky ooze of nihilism and worthlessness. There was no Universe, no Force, no God. No higher power of any kind. Everything was haphazard and random. Life, ultimately, was meaningless, and if life was meaningless, then clearly, so was I. I sat at the edge of our bed and began to form the words that my husband had already been saying for many years: *I don't believe in God. I don't believe in God.*

The statement felt awkward and taboo, like the first time you say a swear word. But the more you say it, the more you grow accustomed to it.

I don't believe in God.

And then it becomes easier to say.

I don't believe in God.

CHAPTER 5

Down the Rabbit Hole of Atheism

When I had prophetic dreams, I felt as if a faucet had been turned on to full blast, flooding my entire being with spiritual experiences and feelings of superiority. I considered myself very special because of those dreams, and no matter what mess my life was in, I felt I still had a secret knowledge, something very few others had. Over the years, however, the dreams slowed to the sad trickle of a dripping faucet, so fear began to set in. From my youth onward, I had crafted my self-image on the foundation of these dreams and experiences, which left me with one uncertain thought: *If I didn't have the dreams, if they were part of me only in the past tense, who, then, was I in the present moment?*

The answer was unnerving: I was a spiritual has-been, back to living out my days sitting in an office cubicle, making expensive PowerPoint presentations, while paying someone else to care for my children. My children were the only thing that gave true meaning to my life.

Maybe I wasn't as special as I'd always thought.

In the past, if feelings of mediocrity set in, I could just change jobs, change boyfriends, change home states. But marriage, parenthood, and homeownership made it impossible to skip town and reinvent myself. I was forced to stay put.

The gloom deepened. I began to think of skills or hobbies that I could pick up to bring back those old feelings of specialness. I didn't want to go back to anything I excelled at pre-motherhood because I'd just get depressed that I wasn't as good at them as I had once been, which meant I took trail running and weightlifting off the table. I thought about book writing, but with many unpublished fantasy fiction manuscripts under my belt, I knew the writing process was a long slog, and I didn't have the interest or energy to go through it only to be rejected again.

I needed something I could learn and study on my own in minimal time with minimal equipment or money spent. Finally, I settled on math. I always liked the hard sciences and mathematics, but I was never a natural at them. Although the upper reaches of science were immediately out of my reach, I could bone up on the dusty old math skills that I liked in school and had mostly forgotten. I bought a math book for adults online and was delighted when it arrived a few days later. Forget subjective experiences! I could study hard facts and get a little smarter and defeat the feeling of having a scattered mom brain. I wouldn't feel so drab—a boring mother of two young children.

However, my happy bubble popped soon enough. I had finished a math lesson and caught up with Pat in the kitchen and explained my plan to get smarter.

"Interesting," Pat said. "You know, though, there have been studies recently that show your intelligence is fixed. There's not really a way you can increase your intelligence. You can get better at some math skills, but that's not the same thing as becoming more intelligent." (Incidentally, advances in neuroscience show that this is not the full picture. Though the brain may not be as elastic as it is in its prime, new skills, habits, and abilities can be developed at any stage of life).

Even to this day, Pat has no recollection of saying this, but I do. Consider it a negativity bias—my habit was to focus on the bad over the good, and this one stuck. There wasn't a point to studying math if I couldn't increase my intelligence. Just knowing some basic algebraic formulas wouldn't make me feel special. Crestfallen, I dropped the math book in the trash.

The implications of Pat's comment began to seep into the rest of my life. For one, Pat is the smartest person I know, but he has never made me feel less worthy than him because of that. Nevertheless, I imposed that status on myself. I'd had lots of practice cultivating my fear of mediocrity, and sometimes it's just easier to believe the more negative thing, even if it isn't true.

Meanwhile as a hobby, he was diving into advanced mathematics, neuroscience, and quantum physics. He was learning new data points, and because of his naturally high intelligence, was able to synthesize them quickly. I would hear him have fascinating conversations when friends were over—conversations he'd never have with me. Together, we mostly just talked about work and the kids. I felt so dumb. He seemed to be speeding ahead of me. I was left with a scattered brain, a rollercoaster of hormones, and a growing hatred of having to go to work in an office every day.

I respected Pat so much when it came to his academic side that I began to wonder what else he might be right about. Without the dreams and spiritual experiences, I felt overly ordinary. As time went on without them, I wondered if I'd perhaps misunderstood it all. Maybe it wasn't real in the first place. Maybe it had all been wishful thinking. Pat, as it happened, was becoming more vocal about his atheism. Again, I listened in on the conversations with his friends, and they were all atheists. My failures at learning skills, the job I really didn't want to have anymore, the growing distance between my husband and myself . . . surely there wasn't any rhyme or reason to the workings of the Universe. My life was a crumbling mess, dull and ordinary and so meaningless that I decided that if I wanted to attempt to keep up with my very intelligent husband, I needed to be smart and reasonable. I couldn't hold onto any wishful thinking about my life. All there was in this world amounted to what I could see and touch and feel and hear and taste. Anything else was just a fairy tale for those lucky naïve folks who could take the idea of a deity on faith alone.

Finally, I came to a conclusion about what I'd been working toward for the past decade: the dreams were just my imagination. There wasn't any kind of universal life force. Neither God nor anything like him existed. Sitting on the corner of our bed, one afternoon, I formed the words for the first time and tentatively said them aloud:

"I don't believe in God."

The words felt as strange and forbidden as the first time I yelled a swear word at my older brother when we were kids. But I repeated the words again and again, and the more I said them, and the more time I spent with these new thoughts, the more accustomed to them I became. "I'm an atheist" rolled off the tongue. Soon after, I began teasing my Catholic coworkers with a slice of pepperoni pizza on Fridays during Lent. I began sitting in with Pat and his friends on their philosophical conversations, which made me feel better about myself. I joined in as they joked about the superstitious beliefs that simple-minded Christians held.

No, maybe I couldn't upend my life in order to reinvent myself, but I could destroy my old beliefs and replace them with something that felt sophisticated and cosmopolitan. The superiority I once felt as an advanced spiritual so-and-so was superseded by the superiority I now felt as a high-minded atheist. The sin of pride factored heavily into both ends of the spectrum.

As a spiritual seeker, my beliefs stemmed from my intuition and feelings. I *felt* that I had gotten the inner workings of the Universe pegged: there was a spiritual battle happening, a Universe of light and dark. I was able to see past the crude physicality of the world and know something greater than most people. I felt that dualistic tug-of-war in my soul, and I experienced great things in dreams and the Ouija board and premonitions.

Similarly, much of my atheism was rooted in feeling. *I* was miserable and felt my life had no lasting meaning, so it must stand that the Universe was a cutthroat Darwinian play and ultimately devoid of anything substantial beyond that which we could directly experience with our sensory faculties. If someone had asked me why I had chosen atheism, I'm not sure I could've articulated it more than just based on my own interior struggles.

Since there was no life after this one, there was only one thing left to do: enjoy this life, which I did mostly by drinking with friends and being a mother.

We got pregnant again. Pat and I were still caught in a rising and falling tide, sometimes drifting apart, otherwise happily floating alongside one another, but now I had another life to take care of—a beautiful baby girl. If things didn't work out with Pat, I reasoned, at least I had my son and my daughter. Our marriage had served its purpose by giving me two children, one of each sex.

My views of marriage were clearly utilitarian. Marriage now existed as a paradigm in which to securely raise children. If this marriage were to end and I were to leave Pat, I'd be forced to continue to leave my kids to go to work, something that caused me great pain each day. Most likely, I'd never have the chance to be home with them as I hoped.

I wasn't so romantically deluded that I thought some other man would solve my problems, that if only I found someone better than Pat everything would be fine. If things didn't work out with Pat, I had already committed to never dating or marrying again.

Sex, likewise, had become utilitarian. Previously, I had considered sex to be the greatest gift of my life, but by that point, it was a perfunctory duty that needed to be performed every so often, whether to give me pleasure or to at least keep Pat from getting frustrated and snappy. At best, sex relieved tension for me, and at worst it was a chore that kept my husband happy or happy enough. My complaining leading up to it and my physical withholding during it couldn't have made anyone feel truly loved. We were burdened by work and parenting and the general needs and duties of life. Sex was just another thing in a long to-do list that needed to happen.

The longer things went on, the more withholding I became, pushing Pat away when he tried to hug me or give me a kiss or hold my hand. If I let him do those things, would he push farther and think I'd want to have sex? I didn't want to have sex. I was tired from little hands pawing all over me all day. And besides, the children *needed* me and so had priority. My adult husband, on the other hand, didn't need me in order to survive, and so he had the least claim on my time and energy.

With those thoughts ruling my mind, I continued to do what every successfully married woman had ever advised against: I put my children and my role as mother ahead of my husband and my role as wife. A friend's mother once told me to remember that one day my children would grow up and move away, and what, she asked, will you be left with then? A good marriage? One that you worked on and prioritized throughout the years? Or a shell of a marriage that had been hollowed out by years of neglect and growing animosity? I wanted a good marriage. I wanted that solid foundation. I wanted to love Pat through the years. But I also wasn't willing to do the work to make it so. Having fallen in love with my children, who were so new and beautiful and loving and fresh, who challenged me and grew, who loved me deeply and who would go on adventures with me, I found much more joy and fulfillment there than in the relationship that had given them to me, which had grown stale.

Our experience in these years certainly was not the sacrament of marriage as beautifully expressed in the *Catechism*:

> "Just as of old God encountered his people with a covenant of love and fidelity, so our Savior, the spouse of the Church, now encounters Christian spouses through the sacrament of Matrimony." Christ dwells with them, gives them the strength to take up their crosses and so follow him, to rise again after they have fallen, to forgive one another, to bear one another's burdens, to "be subject to one another out of reverence for Christ," and to love one another with supernatural, tender, and fruitful love. In the joys of their love and family life he gives them here on earth a foretaste of the wedding feast of the Lamb (1642).

Oh, how beautiful, how satisfying of everything that our bodies and souls and minds need when we are joined to another! I longed for this kind of marriage, yet I resisted cultivating such a union with my husband.

The failures in our marriage rested on both me and my husband. Yes, my incomplete and incorrect views on sex caused some large issues in our marriage. I also had a tendency toward a sharp tongue and sarcasm. Pat did things that were troubling as well. He prioritized his business and its success far above spending time with his children and us as a family. He was quick to spend money on things that gave him the outward appearance of success, like a ridiculously expensive sports car with a monthly payment that was more than our mortgage. Sometimes it felt like he was only with us because he had to be, not because he wanted to be. Our hurts, sometimes spoken, oftentimes not, compounded.

Pat and I were not unequally yoked; steeped in narcissism, we equally sought happiness in the wrong things. Even our good deeds toward one another were often founded in our own selfishness—how will this make things better for *me*?

I liked being helpful. I liked being considerate and thoughtful. However, Pat focused so much on himself, he rarely noticed the many things I did around the house or for our family business over the years, which infuriated me. I wanted to be appreciated. I wanted a nod of thanks for all my work.

Without that validation from my husband, any criticism he leveled my way was met with great venom. *How dare he criticize me when he doesn't even acknowledge the good that I do?* My heart continued to harden, not just toward Pat but toward the outside world and toward myself. Progressively, my self-worth became more and more wrapped up in motherhood. My children's successes, even at a very young age, became my triumphs. I was better because of how wonderful they were.

Although my children are quite wonderful, for a person to base their own dignity on someone or something else builds a very shaky, if not downright dangerous, foundation. So on the tough days, when the baby wouldn't stop crying and the toddler wouldn't stop being a toddler, or when I accidentally clipped a tiny bit of a newborn's finger instead of the fingernail, I crumbled. I often bemoaned my motherhood, exclaiming, "I can't do this!" and then collapsed in a heap of tears and mean, angry feelings. Those days showed the cracks, the fault lines, because I was only as strong as the good days.

Having dealt with the fallout of depression as a teenager, I refused to go back there, but it took all my strength to hold the line and not let myself spiral completely out of control. I continued to harden. Functioning was easier with the walls up, but the consequences were far-reaching, and it began to bleed into the place I never wanted it to—my relationship with my children.

Pat would ask me to go out after work for dinner, and I'd say no, that's too difficult with children. How about getting a babysitter? he'd say. No, I haven't been home with the kids all day; I don't want to leave them again. The children would ask to play with the water table. No, I'd say, I don't want to clean up after you. Can we go to the park? No, that's too much effort.

The only thing I seemed able to say yes to was the Promised Land of wine and chocolate at night when everyone else was asleep. Finally, some time for me, the thing I needed most of all but never seemed to get. Alone, with the quiet of slumber around me, I would let my guard down a little, the walls would shrink back for a time, so long as I got the exact amount of time that I wanted, spent in just the way I wanted.

Self-care is important. We need to put on our own oxygen masks before assisting others, as airline attendants tell us before takeoff. But what are the underlying motivations for our self-care efforts? I can speak for my motivations during these early years of parenthood, and they were not entirely wholesome. I desired this time alone at night to try to build back what had gotten chipped away during the day, as if the puzzle pieces broke away from the border in the waking hours and I had to frantically fit them back in before the next day started. I also needed to reach a point of relaxation quickly enough in the short window I had before I had to go to bed or before a baby woke up crying in the night, but it was never enough time, so as time went on, I became greedier and greedier. I fell into a vicious cycle. I'd drink three glasses of wine at night, feel great and relaxed, but in the morning, my patience was thinner than ice in the spring thaw. I was constantly catching up, never ahead, never fully present, puzzle pieces dropping off faster than I could snap them back in. Time to brew that next cup of coffee. When could I have that relaxing drink? How much longer until the kids' bedtime?

Those years, with two children under the age of two, were tough times. Raising kids is exhausting. Had I not been an atheist then, I know it still would've been really hard, but there's a qualitative difference now as a Christian, even with triple the number of children, in how I handle life compared to back then. The difference is staggering. Hindsight gives clarity.

My husband once told me that ancient philosophers would say the only person who could really tell you what the "good life" is—and why it's worth pursuing—were philosophers, because they (presumably) experienced worse forms of life before experiencing the better. The point is that if a person has to ask why the philosophical life is best, then he isn't in a position to make the evaluation, because he hasn't had the relevant experience;

otherwise, he wouldn't be asking that question! At the risk of sounding arrogant, this made sense to me with respect to my conversion: after experiencing the light of Christ and having known what life is like as a non-Christian, it indeed seems nonsensical to ask what form of life is better, even if they are both set up with the same challenging conditions.

During those years, I was tugged between counting down the hours to bedtime and feeling my mortality acutely. I loved my children so badly it hurt, and I hugged my babies close and wept into their soft little shoulders, thinking of them growing up and me growing old. Because what happened after that? True, they would no longer rely on me, I would have my "me time" back, but then there would be death, and all of the time and effort and love I poured into them would be ultimately meaningless as my consciousness "poofed" out of existence at the moment of death and my body turned to worm food.

I feared the thought of nothingness beyond life. I feared the unknown, so I tried to not think too deeply about anything. I resigned myself to the fact that I could do little to improve myself, there was nothing beyond this life, and the main point of living was to get through it with as little suffering as possible. Although I had come to these conclusions, they weren't freeing. I felt trapped. I repeatedly counted how many years left until my children reached adulthood. "Okay," I breathed, "I'll still be in my forties when my youngest turns eighteen. Plenty of life left." As was the case with many of my thoughts and beliefs, my approach to parenting was full of conflicts. I wanted my children to need me forever; I counted down the days until they didn't. I loved being a mother; I was exhausted of being one.

One morning, I woke up with an intense craving for bagels coupled with a slightly queasy stomach. Odd, but alright, I said as I picked up bagels from the store. At lunch I thought about having a glass of wine, but I felt *off.* Could it be? What if I was pregnant? How *could* I be?

No, no, couldn't be, I reasoned, as I poured myself a nice full glass of red, setting it on the counter. The toddlers raced up and down the hallway, screaming and laughing. Toys flooded the living room, dishes in the sink, the floor a mess of food bits and dog fur.

But . . . what if? "Guess I'll take a pregnancy test," I announced, "before I drink this."

Pat made no response, as he typed on the computer, oblivious to his surroundings.

I went to the bathroom and used one of the tests I kept around the house. The children's squeals and chatter grew to an annoying pitch as I stared at the test and watched one line show up in the little window, and barely a breath later, the second line, bold and pink.

"You've got to be kidding me!" I shouted, stamping out of the bathroom. "I'm pregnant!" I dumped the wine down the kitchen drain.

Pat hopped up, laughing, and hugged me around my slumped shoulders. "That's wonderful news!"

Was it? I wondered. I tacked on another three years till I'd have my freedom back, prolonging child-raising years toward fifty. I spent a lot of time processing this change and vacillating between joy at this new life and sorrow over the postponement of the rest of my life. For a time, I was almost embarrassed to announce the pregnancy to family and friends. I felt so irresponsible having three children in three years. What would people say? Who does such an antiquated thing anymore? Could we even afford this?

People asked if we would have any more after this third baby. I always answered with an emphatic *no*. No responsible parent has more than two children, three max, these days. We had to think about vacations, school, extracurricular activities, vehicle and housing size, college tuition, health insurance costs . . . All the big families in my experience seemed dysfunctional. They took sides against one another, they fought, they weren't close. What if I had so many children that I was stretched too thin across them all and no one ever felt like they got enough love from their mother because she was always caring for someone else. Fears that I would create poorly loved, resentful children because of my fertility weighed heavily upon me.

As the pregnancy unfolded, so did other things. Since I was pregnant, I couldn't drink anymore, and while the morning sickness disappeared at the end of the first trimester, a lingering nausea after eating any type of sweets persisted, so I couldn't lean on food as a crutch for any unhappiness. Nevertheless, this baby inside of me filled me with a great sense of peace. The days lengthened as we neared another summer and playing outside in the sun with my two children . . . the tightness around my heart began to release a tiny fragment. I began to feel a growing sense of fatigue at my constant negativity, my biting words, and incessant sarcasm. My children were so *joyful*. Why couldn't I be like that? If it was just because I'd seen more of the world and knew its terribleness, did I really want my children to go the same route and just see the bad as I now had the habit of doing? Or did I want better for them?

Pat's atheism began to unfold as well. He seemed to rather suddenly show a growing interest in the supernatural. Books with fantastic enlightened human brains sketched on the cover, books about the Tao and Buddhism, started to arrive in the mail. Pat asked me about my old spiritual experiences, something I had related to him years earlier when we'd first gotten together but hadn't talked much about since. As I told him once again about the dreams and my former beliefs, I was embarrassed that I had ever believed in things unseen or things unobservable under a microscope or through a telescope. The days of believing in anything beyond this world and my five senses were far, far behind me. I was too smart and too experienced now to go back to believing in any of that nonsense.

And yet, Pat persisted.

He began spending time with the ancient philosophers. First it was Plato and Aristotle, Marcus Aurelius, Seneca. The books arriving in the mail now had photos of ancient marble busts on them, wizened men ruminating over the problems and questions that have pestered humans for millennia.

Soon, these classics gave way to books written by those with "saint" in their names. Augustine, Boethius, Aquinas. And then something rather insane happened.

Pat and I were out for a walk together at the indoor track at the local YMCA—a routine that offered a wonderful time to discuss the family business, finances, future plans, problems, the day-to-day activities while the children played in the kids' area. However, Pat became very quiet for a long while as we circled the track. The depth of his thoughts creased his face, and he suddenly blurted, "Do you know about Jesus Christ?"

I started. *What the heck?* "Um, yeah. Jesus. I know the guy."

"But, do you *know* who he was? Who he claimed to be?" His cheeks were now flushed with excitement.

Harkening back to my years in the Bible Belt, I affected my best southern drawl, "You mean, have I accepted Jesus Christ as my personal Lord and Savior?" I scoffed. "No thanks. He might be what some people need to be a good person, but not me."

Pat nodded and said nothing else. But I watched him

closely. He was still thinking about Jesus, I could tell, and he wasn't walking alongside me anymore on that track, not really anyways.

In the weeks that followed, Pat began to attend church, and not any church, but a *Catholic* church, the pretty little church just a few blocks over from the coffee shop where he spent his mornings doing computer work.

He rarely spoke about it, but something was happening: he was becoming a better husband and father.

I was angry at him for it.

Pat was the one who tore away the final delicate webbing of my original spiritual beliefs. He was the one who set me on the edge of the slippery, muddy slope into atheism. He was the one who made me feel quite confident that the only things in this life were the concrete things we could see and feel and taste and hear and smell and observe. Through him I had become comfortable in my misery.

He was leaving me in that awful dank dark pit, and of all things, he was improving! He was becoming more considerate and attentive. More often, he was putting aside his work and looking into the eyes of our children when they came to him with some exciting idea or news. He wasn't waiting for me to ask (and increasingly pester) for help before he started to help.

But me? In comparison, I was more impatient, more withholding. I felt muckier and more soiled and rumpled than ever, like the space between winter and spring when the earth is ruled by mud and old dirty snow, making everything more awful than it was at the beginning. I hated it. I hated Pat's growth. I hated when he asked if I wanted to go with him to church—any church, my choice. I hated all of it. Most of all, I hated myself. But suddenly, slowly, there was something else I began to hate: my own cynicism.

I wanted to be a more patient, more loving wife and mother. I thought of Jim Carrey in the movie *Yes Man*. That would be nice, I thought, just to be able to say yes to everything. At this point, my anger and stubbornness still created such a strong, thick barrier around my heart, I didn't know how to move forward, so everything was still "no." *But I wanted to move forward*, which was enough for the nearly silent movement of the Holy Spirit to begin, deep down within me, for me to say my first tentative interior "yes" that would change my entire life.

CHAPTER 6

"What If, for 30 Days, You Just Believed?"

I scrolled through my Facebook feed, one post after another. Photos of friends, pictures of coffee, quotes from famous people. Advertisements.

I stopped. *There it was again!*

The same ad that I had seen over and over for the past few months. I hardly ever paid attention to the ads on Facebook, except this one. This one. I didn't even notice the product being advertised, but that didn't really matter; it was the tagline that got wedged in my brain so firmly that it replayed like a chant in my mind without my even really looking at the ad:

"What If, for 30 Days, You Just Believed?"

Since Pat first began his research into philosophy of religion, his reading list transformed, book by book, into a study of Christianity. Simultaneously, this ad began showing up in my social media feed. So, while my husband was becoming more Christian-like by way of his studies, I was slowly being introduced to Christianity by way of my boredom-induced web browsing. The funny thing is that, as far as I'm aware, that advertisement had nothing to do with Christianity, and yet that is how I thought of it, how it kept niggling at me as I sat on the sidelines watching

Pat immerse himself in Christianity and become a better husband and father as he did.

I couldn't help but wonder if there was something to all this Christian stuff. Could it—as wild and wacky as it sounded—actually be true? And even if it weren't true, were there enough potential benefits to living a Christian life, including becoming a better, happier person, that would make the absurdity of organized religion worth it?

What if, for 30 days, you just believed?

I didn't even know what belief actually entailed. Did I need to "accept Jesus Christ as my personal Lord and Savior"? What did that even mean? Could I just read a Bible? Should I pray? What kind of prayers? Did I need to give up my Sunday mornings, get out of comfy pajamas, and actually go to a church?

No, I decided. No, no, no. I couldn't do that, not any of it. And so, as I had many times before, I scrolled right by the ad and left it at that.

And yet . . .

What if, what if, what if?

Meanwhile, Pat thrust himself deeper into Christianity, wrestling with his biggest hangups to a faith in Jesus, and miraculously, Jesus prevailed. Pat set aside his atheism and accepted Christ as Truth. He was eager for me to join him in this newfound belief, but through his years of internet marketing and his experience being my husband, he knew there would be no pressuring me into Christianity. He needed to finesse me a little, present the message in just the right way, and that meant he needed to address my concerns and my disbelief with dispassionate interest.

"You know," he said to me in passing, "I got a book on Kindle you might like. It's called *The Case for Christ* by Lee Strobel."

"Oh?" I said politely.

"It's about an investigative journalist, an atheist, whose

wife converts to Christianity, and he goes on to research Jesus from an historical perspective—he interviews all these experts, including anthropologists and historians and psychologists. Anyways, if you want to take a look, you can read it on your phone."

And then he walked away.

He didn't force me to talk about the book. He didn't make me say I'd read it. He didn't hand me a copy. But he did put the proverbial ball in my court. Which was the smartest thing he could've done. I had, after all, become a "no" person. Had he forced me to make a judgment call right then and there about that book, I would've balked, and the impenetrable walls of Jericho constructed around my heart would have only grown stronger. Instead, he used two evangelization techniques that we ought to pay attention to.

One: often a person can be more persuasive when he can get someone to see that he *isn't* being pushy, but rather that he's allowing the space and genuine freedom for that person to make his own assessment of the Christian faith.

And two: know a person well enough that you can come to a discussion of Christianity from positions he is already interested or invested in.

His brief synopsis of the book did intrigue me. Coming from a family of journalists, being a lover of history and anthropology, *and* having a spouse who seemingly left me in my non-belief? It all worked together to make me want to open the book. Pat hadn't mentioned how the story ended. Did the writer get his wife to de-convert? Or did they coexist without treading on one another's beliefs? Or did he discover his wife was in the same spot as me—with the tiniest smidgen of hope, exhausted by cynical non-belief—yearning for truth?

What if, for 30 days, you just believed?

That week, the advertisement showed up one final time in my Facebook news feed. *This* time, I gave the idea some serious thought, playing around with the idea of a kind of thirty-day faith challenge. That would be long enough to give a real attempt at trying on Christianity. If I got to the end of the month and realized I still didn't believe, then, sure, I might have to eat a little crow, but I would also be in the position to have my atheism strengthened. If I gave this religion an honest try and found it wanting, then I could be even more confident that atheism was true and settle back in, as much as I might not want, into my closed world of no's. If I went through the thirty days and believed in Christ, well . . . Future Christine could worry about that improbability when the time came. Besides, that last option was a bit too frightening to wrap my head around.

If I took this self-proposed challenge, I could spend that time reading *The Case for Christ.* That would, with all my other responsibilities and hobbies, take about a month to get through. But what else? I made a list of other things that people might do if they were going to "believe" for thirty days.

Read the Bible, sure. I could say some prayers here and there. Nothing too committed, something like the old agnostic's prayer: *God, if there is a God, save my soul, if I have a soul.* And I could, as crazy and unpleasant as it sounded, actually, finally, say yes to Pat about going to church. Just absolutely *not* a Catholic church. I'd gotten a good enough idea of Catholicism from practicing family members over the years and being dragged to my friend's parish the morning after all of our Saturday night sleepovers. What I learned on those Sunday mornings was that Catholics try to puff themselves up, make themselves more important, like a middleman to God. If I *was* going to try to develop a personal relationship with Christ, I didn't want any distractions, like a priest or ritual getting in the way. In that regard, the Quaker denomination, a common fixture around our Pennsylvanian hometown, appealed to me. From my understanding, at the Quaker meetinghouses, if a person felt called to speak in a way that may enhance the group's understanding of the Eternal, he or she could stand up and do so. Otherwise, it was rather quiet and peaceful, and if God was anywhere to be found, it would be in peace and quiet.

I didn't want to admit to Pat my experiment, but I also realized that I couldn't be a Christian in secret or I wouldn't be giving the religion an honest try. I was going to have to be open about what I was doing because the one thing I did know from my many experiences of faith-filled Christians, I knew the best ones were bold and outspoken about their beliefs. I would have to be that way too. And even though there would be many things I might not know or understand and other things I might even strongly disagree with, I was going to put my ego aside for the month. I would trust in Christianity, though I couldn't make sense of it and couldn't agree with some of the teachings. Only then could I get to the end of the month and look back behind me, from my safe atheist perch, and say, "See? I gave it the old college try and it was all bunk."

Since part of this Christian experiment was going to church, I had to talk to Pat about it, so we could decide on a church together.

When I haltingly, sheepishly explained my faith challenge to him, he couldn't contain the excitement on his face, but in a flash it was gone, and with great composure, he once again said that I should choose the church. We could try a few different ones.

"But," he said, "I really want you to keep an open mind

about the Catholic Church. I'd like us to all go together at some point."

I opened my mouth to say something snarky, but I surprised even myself by clamping it shut and nodding instead.

"Is there a church you'd want to try first?"

I thought back to the denominations other than Catholicism that I had experienced in my younger years. The Baptists I had known as a child had left a permanent angry scar about the Rapture. The nondenominational church I'd gone to with a friend's family a few times had mood-lighting and T-shirt cannons, which was not my style. Mormonism was too crazy to be an option, and although I had fond memories of going to a summer festival at a universalist church, the only denomination I had any experience in that really seemed to fit me was Lutheran. So, I did a little research into the local Lutheran churches and the pastors at each, finally settling on one that had a decent-looking website. I shot off an email asking for more information and waited for a response.

With the prep work laid, it was time to begin my challenge.

I purchased a cross necklace to wear as a visible sign of my devotion, and on day one of my Thirty-Day Faith Challenge, I woke up early, and with a cup of coffee in hand, sat down in the early morning quiet with a never-before-cracked-open Bible. I read the first couple of chapters from Genesis, jotted notes, and said a fumbling prayer, asking God for faith: "I've been strong enough to hold onto my disbelief for so long, help me to be strong enough to let it go."

My husband's friend, Jared, fresh from a five-year stay in Israel, where he improved his Hebrew skills and lived among many others of his Jewish faith, had just returned to the United States and was staying in our spare bedroom. That morning, when Jared walked down the stairs, and before he even had a cup of coffee in hand, I peppered him with questions from my scribbled notes. A wonderful teacher, he was incredibly patient with my rudimentary questions, and if I asked any silly ones, he didn't let on. I was surprised at how interesting it was to talk about Scripture, and not stale, stiff, or boring as I had expected something so old and archaic to be.

Before work, I clasped the dainty silver cross around my neck. I traced the shape of it with my fingers. It looked so out of place. *This isn't for me*, I thought, and wondered if this was all a terrible mistake. But I had committed to the month. I could do this. It took all my strength to not take the thing off completely or at least hide it under the collar of my shirt, but I resisted and kept it there, laying against my chest for all to see.

As I walked into work, the cross weighed heavily against me, feeling like a blinding neon sign with flashing arrows that pointed out to everyone passing by that I was a fake, trying to pass as a Christian, or perhaps worse, a new convert, raw and ignorant. My pride couldn't hold up. I felt bits of the wall crumble. The little silver cross stayed.

The pastor of the Lutheran church to whom I had reached out emailed me back while I was at work. We set up a time to tour the church later that week.

In the meantime, I followed the same routine as that first morning. In the evening, I read Strobel's book and journaled my thoughts. I said a simple prayer before bed.

For our church visit at the end of the first week, Pat and the kids and I arrived in the parking lot actually on time for an appointment. I had never felt like more of an imposter: children in tow, walking through the halls of that ninety-year-old church, pretending to know what I was doing and what I was looking for. Fortunately, the pastor and the director of the children's ministry were very nice, and I had already promised my husband that I'd give this part of Christianity a try.

As we finished up the tour, my then-two-year-old looked around, eyebrows stitched together. "Where's God?" she asked, and we all laughed.

"What an excellent question," the pastor replied.

As we waved goodbye to the pastor, with promises that we'd be there on that coming Sunday, the usual part of me, that hulking beast known as Ego, disparaged, repeating the same things it had been saying to me for years. "It's embarrassing! It's silly! Believing in something like this. People only need Jesus because they can't believe in God without him. He's just a middle man, a distraction. Besides, believing in God? You don't actually believe in him, do you? No, of course not! You're smart, you're savvy. You don't need him or anyone telling you how to live."

I reminded myself that I hadn't always been without faith of some kind. A decade before I'd had it in spades. Everything happened for a reason, our souls were yearning for betterment, we were to grow and develop in this life so as to inch toward enlightenment. And throughout all those New Age-y type beliefs, I had a belief in some overarching spirit that guided it. Of course, it wasn't the God of the Jews or the Christians, but it was something, and I had believed it. If I could believe back then, why couldn't I believe again? And better yet, believe in something that could help me improve my flaws, become a better wife and mother, rather than me seeking alone in the darkness, failing again and again?

Besides, I couldn't expect to stop feeling so lonely, so

mediocre, so very *blah* if I kept trying the same things. I'd committed to New Age and felt awful. I'd committed to atheism and felt worse.

Yet during all of that, I had found Pat and fallen in love, and I had given birth to three beautiful children, and love abounded within me like nothing I'd ever known before. How was that possible?

"Because of God," my husband told me. "Imagine the love you feel toward your children even watching them in the most mundane instances. That love is just the merest hint of his love. Your love is huge, yet it is a fraction of his."

So I told my pride in no uncertain terms to shut up. I was doing this faith challenge for a month, and that was the end of it.

Since one of the main perks of becoming Christian for my husband was an increase in community and socializing with likeminded people, we said yes to all of the church's activities that were presented to us, including a weekly family-style dinner. Adults could go off and do a Bible study. There was choir practice for older children, and a mommy-and-me music class for younger ones. The idea of sitting around, clapping hands, and singing preschool songs about Christ made me incredibly uncomfortable. I imagined the youth faith activities that I had been dragged to from time to time as a kid and worried it would be overly simplistic and feel cultish and weird. But I RSVPed "yes" to the community dinner and music class, and yet again, I was surprised. It wasn't cultish or weird at all.

Eight children and about a dozen parents attended. We clapped and sang and smiled. The children shook jingle bells. We sang a few songs about how wonderful Jesus is and how loved we all are. I spoke with some of the moms, and it was, very simply, just nice and fun. When we left, I was borderline confused at how much I enjoyed myself. Funny, when you stop being cynical all the time, simple things become fun again.

I decided I had been making my search for faith more complicated than it needed to be, because that night I broke bread with strangers and made friends. I loved my children and sang about God. I worshipped, and it felt right, and it felt good. How much more did I need than that? Were others asking the questions I was? Were they having a crisis or a renewal of faith? Or maybe they were secure in it and there was no reason to think much about it. Could I get to the point of just believing in Christ so completely that I wouldn't have to think about it so much?

Because, right that minute, it was on my mind from sunrise to nightfall. I was even dreaming about Christianity. I felt consumed by this desire to learn more and more. I hungered for a deeper connection to this growing faith, a faith to which I was increasingly and strangely nonresistant. Would this intensity fade? Could I just go to church on Sundays and to the community dinner once a week and not be so totally consumed by my seeking? Could faith live in the background?

And yet, there's a saying, "If it's important, do it every day."

If God is important, *the most important*, then I ought to worship him every day. I should contemplate my faith every day. I should fulfill God's hope that I live my life in accordance with Christ's teachings and his way, each and every day.

The problem was, as much as my cynicism was crumbling, I still didn't have a logical handle on Christ. I was so hopeful that during that Month of Faith Challenge, as I was now calling it, my desire to come to my faith logically would be supplanted by a soulful rejuvenation and refinement of the faith I had within me very long ago, but that wasn't happening. My reasoning faculties required more.

I continued to read Strobel's *The Case for Christ,* and in it, he interviewed eminent New Testament scholar, Bruce Metzger. When asked what all his studies had done for his personal faith, he said, "It has built it. I've asked questions all my life, I've dug into the text, I've studied this thoroughly, and today I know with confidence that my trust in Jesus has been well placed ... *Very* well placed." Perhaps logic and faith could go together, and I didn't need to rely on blind faith to make it through this challenge because, in truth, faith alone wasn't going to cut it for me.

Before even two weeks had passed, I found myself more than halfway through *The Case for Christ.* I couldn't put it down! Each expert, every objection, every explanation, and refutation read as if the book was written just for me.

One night, I rocked back and forth in a chair, nursing my youngest to sleep. The light from the Kindle app on my phone cast a white-blue glow on my baby's face and my hands and the chair and bed. I began reading the section of the book on the Atonement, which was still a huge sticking point for me with Christianity. *How* did Christ die for our sins? Why would he even need to? What, actually, is sin?

These questions and the whole concept of sin dogged me for most of my life. I wasn't perfect. At times, I failed even when I tried not to. And yet, the idea that I was fundamentally and inescapably flawed, per original sin, seemed a cruel and condemning concept that made even the most innocent babe into a villain. That concept repelled me. Further, the notion that my everyday actions piled more sin on top of what Adam and Eve had done seemed even more ridiculous. Who were they to me?

Two ancient strangers with whom I had no noticeable relationship. I felt more condemned by original sin, when I rather wanted to be commended for my desire to spiritually grow. "You say your God is loving," I would challenge Christian friends, "but why is he so judgmental? I make mistakes. You make mistakes, we all make mistakes. So what?"

The "so what" revealed my complete misunderstanding of sin.

Sin, as the *Catechism*, defines it, is "an offense against reason, truth, and right conscience; it is failure in genuine love for God and neighbor caused by a perverse attachment to certain goods. It wounds the nature of man and injures human solidarity. It has been defined as 'an utterance, a deed, or a desire contrary to the eternal law'" (1849).

Besides the violence against God that "big" sins obviously commit, sins like murder and adultery and robbery, it cannot be denied that even our everyday slipups, when combined with one another, over time, cause us and those around us a lot of unnecessary suffering, and hurt our relationship with God.

An example was my sin of impatience, though seemingly small compared to, say, genocide. No matter my intentions or efforts, my patience was not improving. My insides would bubble with annoyance at the sight of someone going too slow ahead of me or my children not being able to find their shoes or my husband taking too long in the store, until I couldn't contain my emotions any longer and they'd burst forth with mean, petty words. After a few hours, when I'd cooled, I would feel guilty for my outburst, and I would vow not to do it again, to be more patient and understanding next time. Still, when the next time came around? The cycle repeated, as can be expected. After all, when "left to ourselves, unaided by grace, we tend toward sin as naturally as a stone is drawn to the earth by gravity, as readily as a boat that is caught in the strong current is carried downstream."[3] My frustrations with myself grew.

In and of itself, this issue of mine may not appear overtly harmful. I wasn't abusing anyone or physically harming someone, but I was still causing hurt and pain, most often to the people closest to me, which eroded those relationships. Could they trust I wouldn't explode? Were they scared of what my reaction might be? Sometimes I could see it in their faces—the expectation that I would snap—and that made my guilt grow and grow.

There seemed to be no end to this cycle. I couldn't just brush off this flaw of mine. It was causing real problems, and I couldn't pretend that they'd magically be fixed someday or that finally my same efforts after each outburst would produce different results. Besides, in the meantime, what did I expect everyone around me to do? Just accept it and deal with this character flaw? And yet, I *did* brush it off as merely an unavoidable part of my personality, just something to be accepted. "If you don't love me at my worst," to paraphrase Marilyn Monroe, "you don't deserve me at my best." I wasn't perfect and I wasn't going to be perfect. Again, so what? Just deal with it.

And yet, let's be real. I was undeniably thinking and acting wrongly. My impatience, both the petty words spoken and unspoken, caused hurt. Interiorly, left mostly unchecked, it put me in a mindset that wasn't compassionate or gentle or kind. So, although my imperfections and how I conducted myself can be perfectly encapsulated in the catechism definition of "sin," I could not acknowledge that, because it meant knowing the truth of myself: my current condition and my ultimate end. Those truths are quite uncomfortable. They also rebel completely against the narrative of the post-Christian world in which we live, that we are each living our own truth, just trying to live our own best lives, and we shouldn't judge others. Live and let live, no matter the consequences.

Years earlier, when I studied Judaism, I came across the Greek word for sin, *hamartia*, which in a literal translation means to miss the mark, as an archer might miss the bullseye. This definition seemed less condemnatory, something that I could wrap my relativistic mind around. Perhaps the idea of sin wasn't so bad, I thought, so long as it was couched in such a way. I didn't feel I was actually doing anything *wrong*, but rather failing to live up to the ideal. I'm not entirely to blame. You see, I took a shot but I missed the mark. That definition became a convenient way to make me feel as though I'd matured, without taking much responsibility for myself.

Since becoming Catholic and coming to a clearer understanding of human nature and the teachings of sin, I've heard from many mothers of wayward children who talk of sin in the same way I once did, which I completely understand. Taking ownership of one's flaws is a scary thing, and on the surface it seems judgmental. However, and this is a big "however," God does not ask us to sit in judgment of ourselves and never see the light of his love, because to do so would be awful. Rather, he asks us to see our sins as they are, so that we can understand our need for a Savior, and then he can pull us out of our old ways, our dead selves, and make us into new men and women in Christ.

All he is asking of us is to see things for how they actually are. First: a broken world, a human race, lost to its spiritual and physical gifts, with misaligned steering that veers us constantly off course. Second: a perfect and loving Creator who has taken our sins and our doomed nature, rescued us from ourselves, and who gives us a gratuitous gift of himself, inviting us to an eternal friendship with him that we are in no way owed.

As the evidence compounded in the balance for Christ and everything he did, another thing became increasingly obvious to me: if Christ was a historical person who died and rose from the dead, I needed to rethink why he did those things. Based on Christ's own words, undeniably, it was for our salvation. Although I was as yet incapable of wrapping my mind around the exact details of how that all worked, Calvary began to make sense. Obviously, humanity, after millennia of sinning, had collected red in its ledger. Look at the broken world! Of course it had! And then I took a good, hard, awful look at my own ledger. It was a red and bloody mess.

Of course, Christ, the Son of God, the Spotless Lamb, would have been the only sacrificial offering worthy to blot that red out, once and for all. It was true, I realized: he *had* died for our sins. He died for my sins. He died for me.

The magnitude of this realization was staggering.

This truth was not just a small door or passageway to my walled-off heart that opened, no!

Instead, after years of the Holy Spirit pacing around my heart, after the thundering of his trumpets, finally, yes, *finally*, the entire wall came crashing down.

I couldn't move. A long time passed. The light of my phone dimmed, then went dark. With the blue glow gone, I sat rocking my sweet infant—a warm soft bundle of love, with the room perfectly still and quiet. Right there, in nearly the very same place where I had first tentatively said that I didn't believe in God at all, came another tentative declaration: "I am a Christian. *I am a Christian.*"

I sat marveling at those words for some time, and then the concerns for Future Christine that I had brushed off at the beginning of my thirty-day faith challenge came rushing back. If I'm a Christian, then what next? How do I tell Pat? Do I tell my parents? Do I tell my friends? Do I make an announcement to the pastor? I had no idea what I was supposed to do, but whatever it meant to actually be a living, breathing, all-in believer scared the hell out of me.

I thought back to when we had gone on our tour of the Lutheran church a few weeks prior. The pastor, upon hearing our faith background had been very loosely Catholic, said that we're all heading in the same direction, we're just in different boats. The Lutherans in one boat. Catholics in another. And yet, each of us, he said, individually has our own boat too. There are 7.5 billion boats in these ethereal waters. Many people don't even know they've set sail at all, or they wouldn't believe it if you told them. I certainly wouldn't have, just a few months prior to all of this.

I thought about the parents in the music class. The moms and dads singing along in their boats, me in mine. Perhaps we were all in the same general congregation of boats as Christians and then grouped together again by denomination as Lutherans or Catholics or Presbyterians and so on. Due to the nature of my quest, my boat pushed the speed, the waters splashing with the quick, fervent movement of my craft. I had passion and purpose to my travels, and even now, I know what I will see and learn might be different than my fellow travelers, simply because I wasn't raised up in this knowledge but came to it willingly and with many, many questions.

In the following days, after my stunning realization, I continued to read the Bible and study and watch documentaries and go to church on Sunday. I felt less angst about my choice in the flavor of Christianity, and less concern that mine was different than my husband's. If Pat felt called to be Catholic, that was fine. His choice had no bearing on me. I had found something in the Lutheran denomination, and it was working for me. I had gotten myself to the waters of Christianity. Pat was there, too, though in a different area. That, I thought, was good enough.

My opinion shifted when Christmas Eve rolled around and something in Pat changed.

CHAPTER 7

Embracing the Universal Religion

Growing up, Christmas Eve was wondrous. My dad drove me and my brother around town to see the holiday lights. Back home, Mom worked at breakneck speed to transform the ordinary into the magical. The plain wooden table, the basic cream walls of the dining room, would be completely different upon our return. Walking from the hallway through the kitchen was like stepping through C.S. Lewis's wardrobe, from everyday to winter wonderland. Each year, Mom outdid herself, a new theme, new wonders. Everything was truly magical.

So, when we began having children, I was determined to continue this high-bar tradition set by my parents. I worked furiously every night in the weeks between Thanksgiving and December 24 to create the magic in our home.

Pat hated it.

He didn't hate the *idea*, though, but rather the way I was going about it. For weeks, I almost entirely ignored him as I crafted, planned, and prepped, waving him off, barely looking up from my work to say hello, give a kiss, go on a date.

"This isn't the point of Christmas," he said one night as I yet again ignored him to string marshmallows on fishing line in my plan to turn the dining room into a snowing candy wonderland.

How dare he minimize my hard work! I seethed. But I carried on. Christmas Eve arrived, and between nap time and diaper changes, I slaved in the kitchen, put the final decorating touches on the table, and looked forward to a nice night at home with the family, finally getting to enjoy all my efforts. Even the weather cooperated by providing freezing rain and snow in the late afternoon for a white Christmas.

Pat walked into the kitchen. "I'm gonna go to Mass tonight."

Flushed and sweaty, I spun around from my place in front of the stove where I had been stationed for the better part of two hours. "WHAT?!"

He repeated himself.

I stared, slack-jawed, at him. He'd seen all the work I had done. He knew how important this was, and yet he decided to leave in a worsening winter storm to go to church? "But, but, but we're going to the Lutheran church tomorrow. And dinner is soon! What would possess you to do this?"

"I have to go. I'm sorry. I'll be back right after. It'll still be early enough for dinner."

And then I watched my husband, who has terrible eyesight at night and especially hates driving in snow, risk his safety and my wrath by walking out to his car and driving off to a nearby Catholic church for Christmas Eve vigil. I was flabbergasted. How could anyone feel so strongly about his faith that he would go not once but twice to a Christmas service, especially in these driving conditions and after all my hard work? I scrambled to adapt the meal, all the while thinking that if anything was overcooked, dried out, or chewy, it would serve him right. *That'll teach him to mess with my plans. And on Christmas Eve of all times!*

He made it to the church and back just fine, but afterward, something was different; *he* was different. I struggle to put my finger on it now, but whatever interior conversion he had been moving toward during those months of reading about Christ and attending Mass here and there, culminated in that Christmas Eve at St. Agnes Catholic Church. Lutheranism wasn't going to work for him, and despite my petty anger over his daring to leave, it made me rethink Catholicism for the first time. It had been a seemingly small battle, but at that point the war for his soul was won. I didn't understand the implications of it all then, but I knew something was different, and I was willing, out of sheer curiosity, not unlike buying a ticket to a freak show, to take a look at what might drive him to such madness.

One evening in January, I came downstairs after the nightly bedtime routine with the kids. "Want to watch an episode of the *Catholicism* series with me?" he asked. I looked at the TV.

The show had just begun, and the music and visuals were beautiful enough to hook me on the spot. "Sure," I said, and got comfortable on the couch with a glass of wine.

As it turned out, the hour-long episode was fascinating. Pat hadn't mentioned Bp. Robert Barron before, but his tone was so joyful, so soothing, the cinematography beautiful and the music haunting that, along with Pat's Christmas Eve experience, the Catholic faith started to become a viable option, but I struggled with the idea of abandoning my Lutheran path. I'd made the effort in my faith journey to find a good church. Did I really need to go further? The children and I were invested in the Lutheran church. The pastors had set us up with a host family to befriend us and show us around, the date had been set for my baptism and the children's, we were heavily involved in the weekly family dinners, music classes, and the adults-only pub theology.

Ironically, my deepening involvement in the Lutheran church's culture provided my final push toward Catholicism.

Every other week, a group of adults from the Lutheran church got together at a local pub where the associate pastor led a question-and-answer session, with a variety of questions and topics. Despite Pat's attraction to Catholicism, he was still willing to show up and be involved in the church I felt comfortable in. I had been unable to attend the few times that Pat had gone to these bimonthly events, but now we finally were able to line up a babysitter. I was excited about getting out of the house for a bit in the evening, even though I really had no interest in sitting through hours of heavy philosophical discussion, but Pat promised it was fun and the conversation light, and suggested we invite a few other friends with us. So, we reached out to our Jewish friend Jared, who was still staying with us, and invited an evangelical Christian husband and wife who had been praying hard for our conversion, to come along as well.

Unfortunately, once we ordered drinks and food and settled in, made introductions and toasted a nice evening out, the promising pleasantness of the night came to a swift and eye-opening stop.

The pastor took out a few notecards from her bag, flipped through them, and landed on one. "Ah, this is an interesting idea. 'Do you think,'" she read, "'it's a problem that we refer to God as a 'he'?"

The shoulders of our evangelical friends visibly stiffened, but they spoke calmly as they explained why it's not a problem at all; indeed, God referred to *himself* in the masculine. Others in the group started down a trail of gender fluidity and promotion of homosexuality and transgenderism that seemed a far offshoot of what we should have been discussing.

Then, somehow, impossibly, the group turned toward critiquing the Israeli state and Judaism, making egregiously false claims about the Jewish people, insinuating the Christian God is not the same as the Jewish one, and that modern Jews were directly responsible for the death of Jesus and deserved the Holocaust.

Jared, who had spent years studying his people and religion, staying abreast of politics, and actually living in Israel, took a deep breath, and on the exhale began batting down each of the jabs, insults, and falsehoods. Despite the rising passions and the direct attacks upon him, Jared remained quite articulate. The others, however—my jaw dropped. The vitriol coming out of their mouths was stunning and awful. Worst of all, the pastor did nothing to mediate this destructive conversation! Instead, as the evening's conversation continued to spiral downward, she pulled her phone out of her purse and abruptly stood. "Babysitter is calling. Gotta go!" With a nervous chuckle as she dashed out of the bar, she added, "Play nice!"

But the damage had been done. Beyond their poor behavior, their doctrinal confusion showed a severe lack of theological consistency with some modernist heresies thrown in! I still didn't know much about Christianity, but I knew that I was seeking consistency and tradition and solid teachings.

As Catholic philosopher Peter Geach writes, "[The modernist Christian's] teaching will be a matter of learned conjectures intermixed with such fragments, few or many, of the old tradition as he chooses still to believe.

He may choose to believe all this; but he will scarcely persuade a rational outsider, and he can claim no authority that should bind the conscience of a Christian."[4]

What I witnessed smacked of this modernism, with which I wanted no relationship, and the behaviors on display were more akin to those of "Christian" behavior I had seen as a youth that made me run far from Christ.

Overall, the entire evening was a wreck, and though I wasn't, at that moment, able to agree to move completely away from the church and denomination I'd initially chosen, I *was* ready to put aside the stubbornness and laziness that kept me from exploring Catholicism.

Pat and I watched another episode of the *Catholicism* series. Completely opposite of the pub theology experience, here at least, peace and truth exuded from the television screen. In this episode, Bp. Barron explained *transubstantiation*, that miraculous changing of ordinary bread and wine into the actual Body and Blood of Christ. I had no idea about any of this. I wondered why, in all the times I'd gone to my friend's Catholic church growing up, I had never heard this, not even in my religious studies minor in college. It dawned on me that if the Holy Spirit was really changing the substance of the bread and wine, and if Jesus was really coming to Earth and to dwell in a very intimate and special way within the people partaking in this miracle, well then wow! And of course, Catholicism!

Suddenly, it all made sense: the opulence of the church, the gold, the marble, the candlesticks, the incense, the rituals, the dress, the words, the movements, the sitting and standing and kneeling . . . if Jesus was really, actually present in the church, then of course the Catholic Church exists as it does, and most importantly, of course the Church is true—and *only* the Catholic Church is true through and through (though there can be kernels of truth in the other faith traditions I had spent years chasing). Jesus, after all, doesn't do this anywhere else! And if this was the case, if I was really going to follow Jesus, if this special thing only happens within the Catholic faith, ought I not go there, too?

As the episode came to a close, Pat asked me again to go to Mass with him. This time, before my ego could get in the way, I said yes.

And there, the following morning, among the cool white marble and detailed stained-glass windows and golden candlesticks, and warm wooden pews, the slow, deliberate movements of the priest, the Scripture readings, the vestments, the quiet . . . everything I'd learned the previous evening, my searching for Christ, the opening of my heart to the workings of the Holy Spirit . . . it all clicked. If I hadn't already been on my knees when the bells rang three times, proclaiming the changing of the bread and wine into the Body and Blood of Christ, I would've fallen to them. I understood, and I knew getting to Christianity wasn't enough. Jesus was here. He was *right here*, and I needed to go all-in.

I was Catholic.

And I was terrified.

Becoming Catholic was against everything I had told myself for years. It was against how I had acted, thought, and related to Catholics and Catholicism. I really didn't know what it meant to actually be a Catholic—I barely knew how to be a minimum "mere Christian," but at work later that morning, I drafted up an email to the Lutheran pastor, expressing my sadness over the pub theology evening, as well as explaining that through my continued study of Christianity, I could no longer be brought into the faith through their church. I was going to be Catholic.

For several long minutes, I stared at the message on

the computer screen. Once I hit send, there would be no going back. I would have to keep moving forward . . . as a Catholic. I thought again of my experience at Mass, reliving the half an hour spent feeling like I was on some other spiritual plane, and sent the email. It was done.

Next, I found the tab on that same Catholic parish's website about faith formation and sent another email, this time to the religious sister in charge of the program. Before the day was out, Sr. Mary responded, and we set up a time to meet a few days later in her office at the church.

We arrived at the parish office that cold winter morning and glanced up at the sky—a clear blue that only seems to come with the most frigid days. I felt that sky perfectly fitting for the day—the clouds in my mind and heart had been cleared away, and the sun was shining in.

A small gray-haired woman in a habit the same color as the sky greeted us at the door, and with a large smile and a laugh, invited us inside the old Victorian-style home.

Sr. Mary led us up the narrow creaking stairs with apologies. "We're building a new office, but for now," she shrugged and chuckled, "this is where we are!"

I kept my coat on and my hands in my pockets as we sat in a cramped room at what looked like a school lunch table. Briefly, Sr. Mary asked us to explain why we had made the appointment, why we wanted to become Catholic. She listened intently as we told the long journey toward Christianity and then the shockingly sudden turn to Catholicism.

Then she asked some questions about personal information, about our children, if we'd been married before, about our marriage now. For Pat, the logistics were straightforward. He was baptized Catholic and so simply needed to be confirmed. And since he had been studying Catholicism so furiously for months, Sr. Mary was confident that Pat could be confirmed without coming to each week's meeting of the RCIA—Rite of Christian Initiation for Adults, as I came to know.

For me to be confirmed in the Catholic faith, on the other hand, would take some time. I had very little education in Catholicism. I definitely needed to attend the RCIA meetings. I was also very late in coming in. Lent was almost upon us, which meant the preparations were almost over for those entering the Catholic Church at Easter. I was far behind in studies and preparation.

The process was not as simple as it would have been at the Lutheran church, and yet, I didn't mind. It didn't seem onerous at all, and since I had spent so many years mocking Catholicism, if now I had to wait and work a bit to come into full communion with the Church, that seemed fitting. I had pushed far too long for things to be done "my way," which had failed. I was at peace following the lead of the Church.

Next on our conversion to-do list, we spoke about baptizing our children. We'd need to take a class, and we'd need to name godparents.

Pat and I looked at each other. *Godparents?* No one we knew was a practicing Catholic! How were we going to find someone willing to step into that role?

At the end of the hour, Sr. Mary gave us a folder filled with papers, a textbook, the schedule for the RCIA meetings, and a smile—she was very happy we were there, and she would help us.

Stepping back out into the bright winter day, the temperature wasn't much different than inside, and I felt *good*. Really good. For the first time in years, I was buoyed by something other than my own efforts. I could feel God working within me, and I was filled with joy at finally being on the right path.

"Okay!" I said to Pat as we stood on the uneven sidewalk outside.

He smiled back. "Okay."

We walked back to the car, hand in hand. Besides paperwork and scheduling, all we had to do was figure out what living a Catholic life actually entailed, which is where it got tricky. It's one thing to wear a cross necklace and to go to a church where no one knows you yet, but what about friends and family? How do you tell them? How do you act around them? What about our lives would change?

Obviously, I've done a lot of stupid things in my life, and I've owned up to a good chunk of them to my parents. However, planning to tell them I had decided to become Catholic was beyond scary.

But telling my mother was easier than I'd expected. I had been letting her into my life more as the weeks of my faith challenge had gone by. She had been visiting during one of our first Sundays of going to Mass so the fact that I was seeking wasn't a surprise. She seemed genuinely happy for me, which went a long way in helping me push forward with my decision.

Confiding in my father about my conversion was a whole other beast entirely. To tell the man whom I respect and value so much, and who had made it no secret his dislike for organized religion generally, and Catholicism specifically, even thinking about how to approach that conversation overwhelmed me. I knew there were two things I needed to express to him about my newfound faith: first, the conversion wasn't solely of heart or wishful thinking. I had explored all the angles. I had come through a long road of belief and unbelief, and all those many roads of research, philosophy, and logical thought converged on Catholicism. In short, I wasn't walking into the Church blind. Second, I was confident in my faith and that I had made the right choice, coming to Jesus. I could not be faint of heart. Catholicism, truly, is for the brave.

These were both massively difficult to convey. As a new convert who hadn't even begun RCIA classes, I certainly didn't know much about the Faith, and what little I did know, I struggled to express eloquently. I also wasn't very confident. Yes, I'd had a conversion; but I was working on my relationship with God and my trust in him was still fragile. Fresh and raw, a tender shoot rising from the soft soil in a spring garden, I wasn't yet prepared for torrential rains or scorching heat, which is akin to how I envisioned the inevitable phone call to my father. I walked around in a constant state of cold sweat and stomach flips for a week before I worked up the nerve.

"Enough!" I told Pat one afternoon. "Watch the kids. I'll be back." And before I could overthink it any further, I stomped out to my car, shut myself inside, and called my dad.

With shaking voice, I explained everything—the years of misery as an atheist, my final prayers for coming out of entrenched skepticism, my faith challenge, the research—and how these things worked together, in both my heart, and very importantly, my mind to convince me that Catholicism was true. I'd be getting baptized at Easter.

To my great surprise, he listened, and he responded with gentleness. He simply said that it was good I had done my research because "blind faith is no faith at all." It's better to find the answers than to force yourself not to ask them in the first place for fear you're not being faithful enough.

For the hours I spent agonizing over this conversation, the phone call lasted less than ten minutes. Afterward, I felt shaky and sweaty as I reentered the house.

"How'd it go?" Pat asked.

I shrugged. "Fine. Better than I thought."

"Well, that's good."

"Yeah, yeah, I guess it is." I still felt tender and raw, and I felt different, not completely in a good way. I had made steps forward from which I could not retreat. I had survived telling my father, which I considered my biggest hurdle.

My trust in God bloomed. I wasn't scared to wear the cross necklace anymore, even when coworkers started to ask about it. As a family, we made the sign of the cross before meals, even when we ate out at restaurants. We began to go to Mass each Sunday, even when we didn't particularly feel like it. I practiced learning all the prayers and memorizing the sequence for the rosary. We made friends with other Catholic couples. I took religious books around with me and wasn't shy about pulling a Bible out of my bag to read on the park bench while my children played.

RCIA classes continued, and even though I would need to continue RCIA classes the following autumn, Sr. Mary and the parish priest did all the behind-the-scenes work so that on that sacred night before Easter Sunday, dressed in white, I stood outside the old stone church and felt humbled and excited and in awe as I stepped into the darkened sanctuary, one of just a few others who didn't have candles yet lit to signify the light of Christ living within them.

Pat and my mom sat on either side of me, along with a couple of friends. We moved through the sacred liturgy of Easter Vigil Mass, and in that long two-and-a-half hours, I felt my own salvation history play out, the years of yearning for God, the long years of searching for him in all the wrong places, the agonizing years when I stopped looking for him, and the joyful times when he came looking for me.

Then, with my husband's hand on my shoulder, I was presented to the Church. I rejected Satan and his empty promises. The baptismal waters poured over me, my forehead was christened with oils, and I was made new. The old me wasn't merely refashioned. No! God took that person who was spiritually dead and gave birth to me, made me someone wholly new, wholly cleansed. The words of C.S. Lewis in *Mere Christianity,* which I had read along my journey, came alive: "Christ says 'Give me All. I don't want so much of your time and so much of your money and so much of your work: I want You. I have not come to torment your natural self, but to kill it . . . I will give you a new self instead. In fact, I will give you Myself: my own will shall become yours.'"[5]

I was God's now, and I was new.

In those moments, I felt so close to God, so alive, I thought I might never sin again.

We returned home and ate a beautiful cake my mom had decorated, and in the morning, celebrated Easter by taking the children, who had been left at home with my dad the night before, to Mass, enjoying candy, having fun with an egg hunt in the beautiful and unseasonably warm spring day, and reveling in this new life.

On Easter Monday, the weather turned. Snow fell as we all walked into the parish yet again, this time with my dad alongside us, to have our marriage blessed in the Church after Mass in a small ceremony in Father's office.

But that wasn't what happened.

The readings and the message in Father's own homily inspired him to help us proclaim the gospel in a different way: by having us get married in front of everyone attending daily Mass that day.

So, whereas Pat and I had gotten civilly united in wine country with the whole shebang—the dress, the music, the cake, the food, the honeymoon—here at this impromptu wedding in front of fifty strangers and no big celebration, we were brought to tears of joy. *This* wedding ceremony was the sacramental marriage that would carry us to heaven. *This* union was the bond we both craved for so long but had no idea how to actually create. After this, there would be no attempts at giving up. No talk of divorce or separation. Rather, there would be sanctifying moments and prayers and mortification, and deep love and a common purpose of getting each other and our children to heaven.

From that day to this day, we have never fought or argued or disagreed again.

Just kidding! We had both been called by Christ to join—or in Pat's case, rejoin—his Church. That fundamentally changed both of us. Convalidating our marriage changed us, but as humans and concupiscible tendencies and sinful natures go, we still argue and fight and disagree—but the goalposts have forever been repositioned and staked permanently. The purpose isn't to be right, but to guide each other to the Right. Sometimes we take turns watching the children so we can run ourselves through the confessional for a proper cleansing.

Even made new in our Catholic faith, life is *not* easy. Faith requires me to sweetly yield at times when a bitter word would be more immediately satisfying. It requires Pat to perform tiresome tasks without complaint that he'd rather leave undone. It requires both of us to work together, as a unified front, to care for our children when our opinions differ, or to grieve the loss of a child to miscarriage or to step in to nurse a relative or friend suffering from illness, addictions, or some other tragic symptom of our fallen world.

Too, Pat and I have had to heal the wounds of our previously secular marriage. We held many wrong notions of what it means to be husband and wife. But in the years since our conversion, we have seen, yet again, a microcosm of salvation history, not just in our individual lives, but in our marriage. At the beginning of our relationship, we had what felt like perfection, an Eden, but there were betrayals and troubles that forced us into a harsher reality. And as in the Old Testament, we struggled in the wanderings of early marriage. Sometimes were markedly better and more prosperous than others but still we were adrift. And then Jesus. And our marriage wasn't just refashioned but made entirely new in light of our Savior. There are still challenges to be sure.

However, faith has simplified our lives. Rather than constantly struggling, as we had as atheists and pagans, with what we should be striving for—the goals we need to be achieving in order to maximize these brief years on this planet before our consciousness goes *poof!* at the end—we now know our life purpose: eternal friendship with God. Our goal now is to get ourselves, each other, and our children to the beatific vision. Secondarily, faith has led us to want to be a light for Christ in this world so that others, too, may come to know the gospel truth.

That isn't to say there aren't confusing times, when I'm uncertain about the best course to take, but in knowing the end goals, and with having the ancient wisdom of the Catholic Church to guide me toward making moral choices on both the little and the big things, takes much of the confusion and the weight off of me. Being Catholic has taken away my prideful need to be an island unto myself. Instead, I rely on the Church and others to help buoy me. My faith and church family have finally given me the connectedness that I had tried to fabricate while being New Age.

Atheists may say the peace and connectedness I feel now is only due to the comfort that belief in the "Bearded Man in the Sky" gives to feeble human minds that keep believers holding onto a transcendent Creator God. Even if that were true, so what? The comfort of our belief in God does not negate the truth. And it isn't all pleasant! This belief in God also comes with a great responsibility. We must do our very best to live up to the moral life to which God tells us to elevate ourselves. And to the Christine I once was, my old self who thought that the Church was a set of rules dreamed up by grumpy men to perpetuate the patriarchy, I'd say I wasn't giving the Catholic faith a fair shake. Just as God gave the Israelites many, many laws in order to separate them from their peers, Christ and his Bride, the Church, give us the moral code for us to flourish. After all, the God who created us surely would know what is best for us, just as a loving mother and father know what is best for their child, even if the child, in the midst of a temper tantrum, would disagree.

Since my baptism there have been challenges in understanding some Church teachings, but I have come to the realization that even if I can't fully understand everything the Church teaches, I have entrusted my soul to her; and having done that, how can I not continue to trust her? There are, after all, very good and satisfactory answers to all of these questions, and in trusting the Church and her wisdom, I was led to those answers, so I needn't proceed from my concerns blindly or fearfully. Life is often quite hard. My faith doesn't fix all difficulties, but it does alleviate how heavily they weigh on me, and even in those difficulties, impossible as it may seem, there is more and deeper joy than even at my happiest in my years without my Catholic faith.

Epilogue

Conversion is not a one-time event. Even Saul, who may have been blinded by the light of Christ on the road to Damascus in one dramatic event and became the apostle Paul, spent years learning the faith, making sure he was teaching the same gospel as the original apostles, and atoning for his past life of sin and persecution.

The roads back into faith, for those who left it, or the roads leading there in the first place, for those who never knew it, will most likely be long and winding, with pit stops, scenic overlooks, and breakdowns. I soon realized being baptized as a Catholic was not a goalpost, but a door opening to the next leg of the journey. What lies ahead may be even harder than my past. I may yet have to pass through even darker parts of the forest, while keeping the light within me burning. My faith asks me to trust that there is real Goodness and Love and Hope, even when the fallen world tells me the opposite. This journey asks us to keep going, even when we don't feel like it, even after the newness of it has worn off, the tires begin to wear, the car gets dirty, and we're tired and wondering why we even started down this path in the first place.

Now, with a proper understanding of Catholicism, this suffering can be accurately framed as my path to holiness, one in which I adhere to the Faith, even if I don't always feel like it because I know that feelings don't negate or affirm the Truth. They are merely a side effect—one that I can't put too much stock in. So when we don't feel like praying, when Mass is boring, when the priest upsets us in the confessional, when the archbishop says something we don't agree with . . . none of those things—or the emotions they subsequently elicit within us—change how Catholic we are. Rather, we trust that Christ formed this Church and that the Holy Spirit forever guides it; and so we continue to practice our faith, even (and especially) when it is boring or hard or dry.

Shortly into my conversion, I started a blog to help me process and retain all that I was learning and experiencing. A reader reached out to me and wrote, "In a couple of years, you may find it very difficult to continue in your faith practice, but keep going anyways." At the time, I laughed to myself. *Oh please*, I thought, *that won't happen to me*. But this woman knew something about the faith journey that I didn't. Even in the Now, when I do go through times of spiritual dryness, I think of her words. She was right, of course. I just was too proud to see it. However, something this person didn't know about me was where I came from: the hopelessness of a life without God and without faith in him. A life of trying to find meaning in creatures, not the Creator. The frustration that I couldn't just make myself be a better person no matter how hard I tried because I would always inevitably fail.

Because this long, long, sad and sick and scary road got me to the point of becoming a Christian, there is nothing—no amount of hurt or suffering—that could get me to turn my back on it. I am a Catholic, and that isn't just an adjective. My faith is a state of being, along with my baptism and confirmation and my continual participation in the sacraments of the Eucharist and reconciliation, in my sacramental marriage, which has left an indelible mark on me. I will never go back to the way I once was.

To quote Westley from *The Princess Bride,* "Life is pain." Of course, life is so much more, too, but suffering is a part of our fallen existence and can't be avoided. But it can be a means to greater holiness, and through a lens of faith I can see and understand and accept that truth. A while ago, I realized I was miscarrying our fifth child, a child we were all very excited to welcome into our arms. In my previous belief system, upon making this horrid discovery, I would have been utterly crushed, pounding my fists against the floor, not understanding why life is so very bad and cruel and unfair. I would have gone toward despair and an anger so deep that it would have seeped into the foundations of our home, threatening to crumble them. However, as a Catholic, the experience was entirely different.

That night, I went to adoration and fell to my knees before the Blessed Sacrament. I said to God, "Look, yes, I'm here asking for a miracle—but most of all, God, I am here asking for the strength to accept your holy will."

I did not get my miracle, but God gave me strength and consolation and healing in spades. Without my trust in him, without my faith, I would not have been able to pick myself up from the bed where I cried for several days, and find myself in a better place, faith-wise, than I had a week prior. In my suffering, I saw God as he loves me. I couldn't have my baby as I wanted him or her, but I had, as always, God's love, and it was beautiful and powerful and sustaining when I opened myself most to it.

We will most certainly suffer, with or without Christ, but as I felt God at work deep within my heart and soul and mind during these past years, and most especially in the painful moments, I can say without any hesitation that all of it—life, suffering, joy, trials, successes, the entire adventure—is always and vastly and infinitely better *with* him. I am a Catholic, and it is now impossible for me to be anything but that—Catholic, beloved, redeemed.

About the Author

Christine Flynn is a convert who writes and speaks about her journey from secular life to embracing the teachings of Catholicism. A transplant to the Midwest, Christine lives with her husband and a growing brood of wonderful children in Wisconsin, where she home-schools, works on the family business, and sings in a cover band.

Endnotes

1 Pew Research Center, "Who Are 'Spiritual but Not Religious' Americans?" *Pew Research Center*, 7 Dec. 2023, https://www.pewresearch.org.

2 C.S. Lewis, *Mere Christianity*, (New York: HarperCollins, 2001), 42-43.

3 Rev. F.J. Remler, *Why Must I Suffer? A Book of Light and Consolation*, (Fitzwilliam, NH: Loreto Publications, 2003), 5.

4 See Edward Feser, "Geach's argument against modernism," https://edwardfeser.blogspot.com/2021/11/geachs-argument-against-modernism.html

5 C.S. Lewis, *Mere Christianity*, (New York: HarperCollins, 2001), 196-97.